THE SOUTHWEST

A GUIDE TO THE WIDE OPEN SPACES

Region

HE

ILLUSTRATIONS BY
ARCH AND MIRIAM HURFORD

A GOLDEN REGIONAL GUIDE

GOLDEN PRESS • NEW YORK

FOREWORD

Everyone knows where the Southwest is, but no two people agree as to what it includes. This book, the first of the Golden Regional Guides, presents to the vacationer, traveler, or interested reader some of the many facets of this appealing land of deserts, mountains, people, places, and events—the Southwest. The book is a guide to the animate and inanimate features of the region, with emphasis on those things most visitors can see and do. It includes sightseeing suggestions, traveling directions, prehistory, history, natural history, Indian lore, and sources of additional information. It is an introduction to the Southwest—one, we hope, that will tempt you to explore further.

Many people have helped in gathering and checking the information in this book. The authors express their grateful thanks to all, especially to Herbert Evison, Sallie Van Valkenburg, Hugh Miller, Bennett Gale, Myrl Walker, and Erik Reed of the National Park Service; and to Stanley Stubbs, Marjory Lambert, and Bertha Dutton of the Laboratory of Anthropology, Santa Fe. Our special thanks are due to Donald Hoffmeister, Hobart Smith, Ira Gabrielson, Alexander Martin, Raymond Carlson, Ray E. Pond, William Carr, Alexander Sprunt IV, and the staff of the Museum of New Mexico. The artists, Arch and Miriam Hurford, have made a rich graphic contribution.

N.N.D.
H.S.Z.

 Designed and Produced by Artists and Writers Press, Inc. Printed in the U.S.A. by Western Printing and Lithographing Company. Published by Golden Press, Inc., Rockefeller Center, New York 20, N. Y. Published Simultaneously in Canada by The Musson Book Company, Ltd., Toronto

CONTENTS

Shalako at Zuni Winter Ceremony

MEET THE SOUTHWEST

THE COUNTRY The Southwest is a region without definite boundaries. Aridity is its principal over-all characteristic. But the region offers amazing contrasts and diversity of climate, geography, and people. Its 465,000 sq. mi. involve nine states and include such superlatives as the lowest land, the biggest canyon, the highest mountain, the driest deserts, the hottest valley, the richest mines, and the oldest towns in the United States. The Southwest is big. But it is also friendly, hospitable, fascinating to live in—full of pleasant surprises, enough for a lifetime.

THE PEOPLE Newcomers have been drifting into the Southwest for 25,000 years, and the tide is undiminished. According to the 1930 Census, the region had then a population of 1,568,200. By 1950 the number had risen to 2,575,250. These figures do not include the hundreds of thousands of summer tourists and winter vacationers, who come for the clear air, sunshine, and unspoiled scenery.

Mt. Whitney, Calif., 14,495
Mt. Elbert, Colo., 14,431
Mt. Massive, Colo., 14,418
Mt. Harvard, Colo., 14,399
Mt. Blanca, Colo., 14,390
La Plata Peak, Colo., 14,340

The Southwest's Highest Mountains

LAND FORMS Except for the eastern plains portion, there is probably no part of the Southwest from which mountains cannot be seen on a clear day. Mountains rise from desert lowlands and from higher plateaus. Much of the Great Basin Desert is located on plateaulands at elevations of 3,000 to 6,000 ft. A wide tongue of the Rocky Mountains extends deep into the Southwest. Many of the low mountain ranges to the south are as much desert as the lowlands that surround them. Other, higher mountains are green forested islands in a "sea" of desert. The map outlines the major topographic areas of the Southwest.

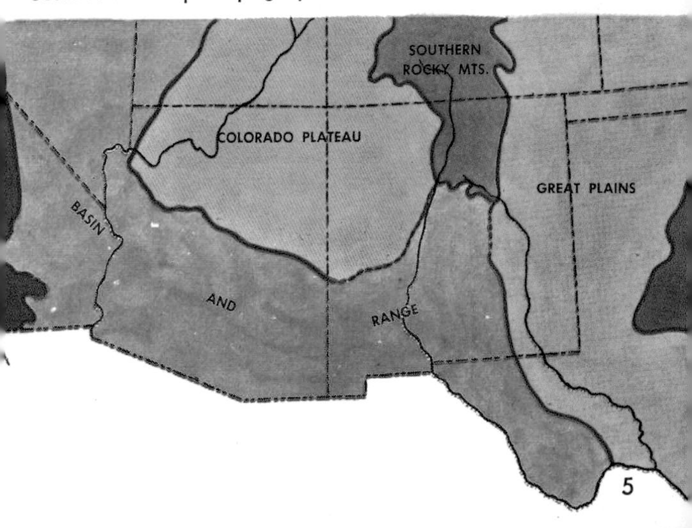

CLIMATE in this land is dry, warm, and breezy. A clear atmosphere, abundant sunshine, and low humidity are typical. Annual precipitation (rain and snow) varies from 1 to 6 in. in the deserts to 30 to 35 in. in the mountains. Much of the moisture falls as spotty but heavy summer thundershowers or as slow winter soakers. Temperatures generally are moderate but vary with latitude, altitude, and other factors. The low south and west parts of the region are hot and dry, the central plateaulands warm and dry, and the mountains cool and moderately moist. Nights are cool. Winter temperatures are cool to cold, depending upon location. Prevailing winds are from the southwest. "Dusters" are common, but tornadoes are practically unknown.

CLIMATIC DATA

City	Elevation, ft.	Avg. Jan. Temp., deg. F.	Avg. July Temp., deg. F.	Avg. Annual Rainfall, inches
Del Rio, Tex.	948	51.9	84.7	18.58
Lubbock, Tex.	3,195	38.8	79.3	18.89
El Paso, Tex.	3,710	43.4	81.3	7.83
Amarillo, Tex.	3,672	35.3	77.8	21.12
Dodge City, Kan.	2,509	30.3	79.9	20.51
Pueblo, Colo.	4,690	29.4	74.9	11.87
Alamosa, Colo.	7,531	16.9	64.1	6.23
Grand Junction, Colo.	4,583	24.0	78.2	9.06
Raton, N. Mex.	6,666	26.2	68.6	15.42
Roswell, N. Mex.	3,600	39.6	79.0	12.07
Albuquerque, N. Mex.	4,943	33.7	79.0	8.68
Winslow, Ariz.	4,856	32.4	77.2	7.83
Phoenix, Ariz.	1,083	49.7	90.1	7.12
Flagstaff, Ariz.	6,894	25.3	65.2	18.47
Yuma, Ariz.	150	55.3	94.6	3.39
Blanding, Utah	6,075	26.6	72.3	12.77
Milford, Utah	4,962	23.8	74.0	8.44
Ely, Nev.	6,000	23.0	68.4	10.52
Las Vegas, Nev.	2,033	44.2	90.5	4.35
Tonopah, Nev.	6 090	30.1	74.6	4.81
Death Valley, Calif.	152	52.0	101.8	2.17

In the Southwest, temperature variations have been recorded from above 130°F. in summer in Death Valley to below −50°F. in the high mountain valleys of southern Colorado in winter.

LASTING IMPRESSIONS Despite the bigness of the Southwest, little things—sights, sounds, and smells—often create the most lasting impressions. Here are some:

Strings of scarlet chili drying against adobe walls.
Golden aspens mantling a mountain's shoulders.
Lithe relaxation of Navajos outside a trading post.
Awkward speed of a fleeing roadrunner.
Massive thunderhead dragging its braids of rain.
Immobility of tumbleweeds banked against a fence.
Line of resigned autos waiting out a flash flood.
Single-file string of steers approaching a waterhole.
Echoes and silences in a great cliff-dwelling ruin.
Bawling of restless cattle at a roundup.
Heady aroma of campfire coffee.
Carefree boys "in the raw" splashing in a stock tank.
Squeal of a fighting, bucking horse at a rodeo.
Wail of a coyote—and yapping of others—at night.
Drum throbs and shrill chant of an Indian dance.
Musty odor of creosote bush after rain.
Bray of a distant wild burro just after sunrise.
Harsh smell of singed flesh at a branding corral.
Sudden pelting rush of a summer thunderstorm.
Unbelievable immensity of the Grand Canyon.
Juiciness of thick steak broiled over mesquite coals.
Stars that you can reach from your sleeping bag.
Splash and tug of a mountain trout hitting your fly.
Tang of enchiladas smothered in chili sauce.

THE MODERN SOUTHWEST

COLORADO
KANSAS
OKLAHOMA
NEW MEXICO
TEXAS
Black Canyon
U.S. 50
PUEBLO
U.S. 85
U.S. 40
U.S. 50
JOHN MARTIN DAM
Great Sand Dunes
U.S. 350
U.S. 160
ALAMOSA
DURANGO
Aztec Ruins
U.S. 285
Capulin Mountain
U.S. 64
U.S. 64-87
TAOS
Chaco Canyon
LOS ALAMOS
Bandelier
SANTA FE
U.S. 85
TUCUMCARI
AMARILLO
U.S. 66
ALBUQUERQUE
U.S. 66
U.S. 60
U.S. 60
Gran Quivira
U.S. 285
U.S. 70
Mountain Time
Central Time
LUBBOCK
ROSWELL
U.S. 70
ELEPHANT BUTTE DAM
CABALLO DAM
ALAMOGORDO
White Sands
AVALON DAM
CARLSBAD
U.S. 87
U.S. 70-80
Carlsbad Caverns
MIDLAND
U.S. 80
EL PASO
RED BLUFF DAM
U.S. 80
U.S. 290
ALPINE
U.S. 90
0 30 60 90 120
One inch equals about 120 miles
Big Bend

Check Your Route

PLAN YOUR TRIP Begin by studying highway maps and pamphlets obtained from railroads, bus and air lines, travel bureaus, chambers of commerce, and state and federal agencies (see p. 120). Auto travelers may obtain tour-aid service from the larger gasoline companies. Much of the Southwest is accessible by paved roads, and modern accommodations are available in most towns. During the heavy summer travel season, try to make overnight reservations in advance or stop early to get a better choice. Obey safety rules and highway signs. If you pull a trailer, find out what hills are ahead.

Off the main roads are Indian villages, spectacular scenery, challenging fishing streams. Be careful never to stop for the night in the bottom of a wash or gully; flash floods give no warning. Keep your gas tank at least half full. When off mapped roads, inquire at each opportunity regarding your route and the condition of the road ahead. If you plan to travel back roads, come well equipped. Use the check lists below.

Car Needs

- Good spare tire
- Good jack
- Basic tool kit
- Reserve water for radiator
- Reserve gasoline
- Ax and shovel
- Tire pump and patches
- Spare fan belt
- Tire chains
- Towrope

Your Needs

- Canteen of water
- Gasoline lantern
- Flashlight and batteries
- Kettle or cooking kit
- Gasoline stove
- "White" gasoline for stove and lantern
- Frying pan
- Sturdy hiking shoes
- Wide-brimmed hat
- Tarpaulin
- Canned foods
- Matches
- First-aid kit
- Snakebite kit
- Pocket knife
- Lip-chap stick
- Sunglasses
- Sunburn lotion
- Compass
- Ball of string
- Blankets or sleeping bag

Camping Locations Are Available in Many Areas

LEAVE THE COUNTRY GREEN AND CLEAN It's good travel manners to enjoy flowers—and leave them for others. Leave all wild animals alone; and keep an eye open for rattlesnakes and scorpions. Don't deface signs, buildings, or natural features. Keep all trash in a paper bag until you drop it into a refuse container or bury it. Always leave a *CLEAN* camp and a *DEAD* fire.

Indians are a proud though friendly people; don't stare or point at them, enter their homes uninvited, or haggle over prices. If you want souvenirs, buy something typical from them or at a trading post.

Help travelers in distress but avoid hitchhikers.

Before starting a hike remember that distances in the Southwest may fool you. Objects appear closer than they are, because of the clean, dry air.

If your car gets stuck in sand, reduce the pressure in your tires to half for better traction.

National parks and monuments are always "open," although accommodations may sometimes be closed. Camping locations are provided in most national forests, in many state and national parks and monuments, and in some state and federal wildlife refuges. Locate campgrounds in advance by referring to p. 120 and to THE CAMPGROUND GUIDE (R. O. Klotz, Campgrounds Unlimited, Blue Rapids, Kan., 1959).

Be careful with fire!

Ghost Town—White Oaks, N. Mex.

DUDE RANCHES AND GHOST TOWNS Guest or "dude" ranches offer a unique, informal vacation in "back country" close to nature. Some are cattle ranches that take in a few paying guests; others may be swank resorts with swimming pools, cocktail bars, and flashy "cowboys" hired as vocalists. Dude ranches specialize in horseback riding, outdoor cooking, and informal rodeos in which guests may participate. Write to chambers of commerce in Southwest cities for information.

Ghost towns usually are mining camps that have "played out." In some, a few families remain, with perhaps a general store and filling station. Others are completely deserted, in ruins, and difficult to find. Check locally for directions and conditions of roads.

Some ghost towns and dates they were founded:

Southeast California: Panamint City 1861, Calico 1881, Bodie 1859.

Southeast Nevada: Tonopah 1864, Searchlight 1897, Nelson 1860, Bullfrog 1905, Rhyolite 1904, Goldfield 1902, Eldorado Canyon 1875, Blackhorse 1900, Alunite, Aurora 1860.

Southern Colorado: Silverton 1873, Creede 1889, Lake City 1874, Eureka 1876, Animas Forks 1875, White Cross 1876, Alpine 1872, St. Elmos 1879, Romley 1870, Hancock 1880, Sherman 1877, Cunningham Gulch 1874, Victor 1891, Burrows Park 1873.

New Mexico: Kelly 1880, Golden 1839, Dolores 1828, San Pedro 1832, White Oaks 1850, Hillsboro 1877, Mogollon 1889, Elizabeth 1868, Kingston 1880, Tyrone, Gold Dust 1879, Shakespeare.

Arizona: Charleston 1879, Contention City 1879, Tubac 1752, Gila City 1858, Oatman 1900, Tombstone 1877, Jerome 1870, Octave 1862, Hardyville 1856, Stanton 1863, Weaver 1862, Goldroad 1863, Silver King 1875, White Hills 1892, McMillanville 1876, Pinal 1875.

For more about ghost towns read: *The Bonanza Trail*, Muriel S. Wolle, Indiana Univ. Press, Bloomington, 1953.

CALENDAR OF EVENTS

(Verify dates locally.)

January—Jan. 6, Buffalo, Deer, and Eagle Dances at Rio Grande pueblos with installation of pueblo governors. Day of Epiphany, Three Kings Feast in Spanish-American villages. Jan. 23, dances, both plazas, San Ildefonso, N. Mex. Bean, Buffalo, and social dances, Hopi villages.
February—Open golf championships, Phoenix and Tucson, Ariz. Spring training, southern Arizona, for major-league ball teams. Cactus show, Desert Botanical Gardens, Tempe, Ariz. Silver Spur Rodeo, Yuma, Ariz.; Fiesta de los Vaqueros (rodeo). Tucson. Plains Indian dances, Taos, N. Mex. Deer and Buffalo dances at Rio Grande pueblos.
March—Stock show, rodeo, San Angelo and El Paso, Tex. Dons' trek to Superstition Mts. and World's Championship Rodeo, Phoenix; Rawhide Roundup, Mesa, Ariz. Indian dances, Keresan pueblos, N. Mex.
March-April—Easter sunrise services, Grand Canyon and Death Valley, Calif. Yaqui Indian ceremonials, Pascua, near Tucson.
April—Rodeo, Douglas, Ariz.; Ride of Desert Caballeros, Wickenburg, Ariz. Festival of Fine Arts, Tucson. Annual Playday, White Sands, N. Mex.; Desert Cavalcade, Calexico, Calif. Many Green Corn Dances.
May—May 5, Cinco de Mayo (Mexican Independence Day) celebrations, both sides international boundary. Ute Bear Dance, Ignacio, Colo. Ceremonial dances, Taos Pueblo. Corn Dance, Cochiti Pueblo. May 15, Feast of San Ysidro in many Spanish-American towns.
June—Cotton Carnival, Lubbock, Tex. New Mex. Musical Festival, Raton. Dances at Taos, San Juan, Santa Clara, San Ildefonso, and Cochiti Pueblos, N. Mex. Ute Sun Dance, Towaoc, Colo.
July—Frontier Days, Prescott, Ariz.; Annual Rodeo, Silver City, N. Mex. Apache Maidens' Fiesta, Mescalero, N. Mex. All-Tribes Pow-Wow and Hopi Craftsman Exhibit, Flagstaff, Ariz. Rodeo de Santa Fe, N. Mex. July 24, Mormon Pioneer Day celebrations throughout Utah.
August—Inter-Tribal Indian Ceremonials, Gallup, N. Mex. Hopi Snake Dances, Outboard Regatta, Lake Mead, Ariz.-Nev. Apache dances and rodeo, Ruidoso, N. Mex. Corn Dances at several N. Mex. pueblos.
September—Labor Day week-end Fiesta, Santa Fe. New Mexico State Fair, Albuquerque. Indian Rodeo, Winslow, Ariz.; Pima Fiesta and Rodeo, Sacaton, Ariz. Harvest dances at Rio Grande pueblos.
October—Navajo Fair and Rodeo, Shiprock, N. Mex. Apache Autumn Festival, San Carlos, Ariz. Papago Arts and Crafts Exhibit, Sells, Ariz. Oct. 31-Nov. 2, ceremonials at most Rio Grande pueblos.
November—Arizona State Fair, Phoenix. Harvest dances in various Hopi villages, Ariz. Encampment of Death Valley 49'ers, California.
November-December—Famous Shalako ceremonials, Zuni Pueblo, N. Mex. Navajo Mt. Way and Night Way ceremonies on reservation.
December—Dec. 12, Nuestra Señora de Guadalupe ceremonials in many Spanish-American villages. Dec. 24-30, Christmas lighting and processions at many Spanish-American villages and Indian pueblos.

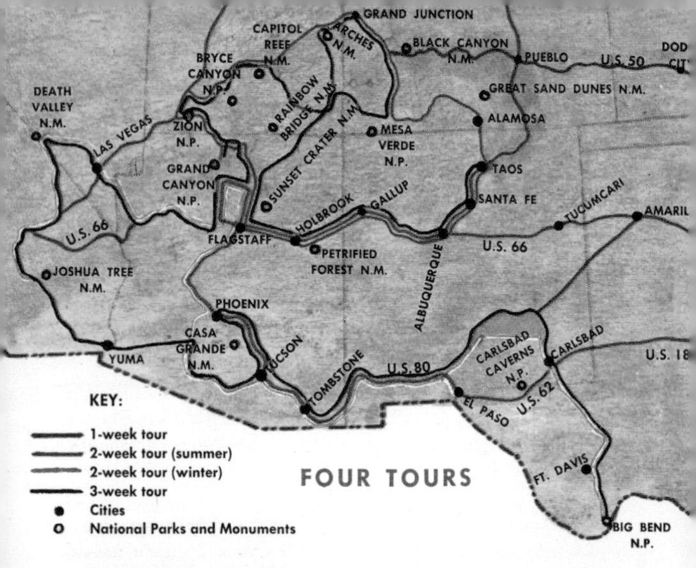

FOUR TOURS

ONE-WEEK TOUR This automobile tour through the heart of the Southwest may be taken in any season; April or October is most comfortable. You can work out other routes from the next two pages or pp. 120-156. Study maps and literature each evening.

First Day: Tour Carlsbad Caverns (4 hours). On to El Paso, Tex., and spend the evening across the border in Juárez, Mexico.

Second Day: It's a day's drive on U.S. 80 to Tucson, Ariz., but you'll have time to see the open-pit mine at Bisbee and stop at old Tombstone.

Third Day: See San Xavier Mission and the Arizona-Sonora Desert Museum near Tucson. Stop at Casa Grande Nat. Mon. and Desert Botanical Gardens near Tempe. Night in Phoenix.

Fourth Day: Take the Oak Creek Canyon branch of U.S. 89, visiting the Jerome Mine Museum, Tuzigoot Ruin, and Montezuma Castle Cliff Dwelling on the way to Flagstaff, Ariz.

Fifth Day: On to Grand Canyon, via Williams. Take the West Rim Drive before lunch, leaving by way of Desert View and Cameron. You can stop at a couple of trading posts, see Sunset Crater, and still reach Winslow in time for supper.

Sixth Day: Take U.S. Highway 260 from Holbrook, cut through Petrified Forest and over U.S. 66 through Gallup, Indian trading center, and on to Albuquerque. You can reach Santa Fe that night.

Seventh Day: There is much to see in Santa Fe, but you should leave before noon. A brief side trip to San Ildefonso Pueblo will get you to Taos in time for a short but interesting afternoon there.

TWO WEEKS IN SUMMER (generally north)

One day: From Albuquerque to Santa Fe, thence to Taos Pueblo.

Two days: Great Sand Dunes Nat. Mon.; Mesa Verde Nat. Park.

Two days: Arches Nat. Mon. and Capitol Reef Nat. Mon.

Two days: Bryce Canyon Nat. Park, Cedar Breaks Nat. Mon.

One day: Zion Nat. Park, St. George, and Utah's cotton area.

Two days: Pipe Spring Nat. Mon. to North Rim Grand Canyon.

One day: Wupatki Nat. Mon., Flagstaff and vicinity.

One day: Meteor Crater, Petrified Forest, Gallup, and Albuquerque.

TWO WEEKS IN WINTER (generally south)

(Reverse route if you come from the west):

One day: Big Bend Nat. Park. Next day via old Fort Davis to—

Two days: Carlsbad Caverns Nat. Park. Via Artesia and Cloudcroft to White Sands Nat. Mon., and on to—

One day: El Paso, Tex., and Juárez, Mexico. Via U.S. 80 to—

Two days: Tucson, Ariz., and Saguaro Nat. Mon., Tumacacori Nat. Mon., San Xavier Mission, and Arizona-Sonora Desert Museum.

Two days: Organ Pipe Cactus Nat. Mon., Gulf of Calif., and thence to Phoenix.

One day: To Flagstaff via Jerome, Montezuma Castle and Well.

Two days: Via Wupatki Nat. Mon. to South Rim Grand Canyon.

One day: Hoover Dam and Lake Mead Nat. Rec. Area.

Two days: Las Vegas, Nev., and Death Valley Nat. Mon., Joshua Tree Nat. Mon., and other attractions of SE California.

A 3-WEEK TOUR OF THE SOUTHWEST This tour of the whole Southwest is best taken in either April or October to avoid temperature extremes. If you must visit the Southwest in summer or in winter, expand one of the trips outlined on p. 15 to fit your schedule. By avoiding the peak of either season, you will miss the crowds and enjoy the country more.

One day: Big Bend Nat. Park, Tex.

Two days: Carlsbad Caverns Nat. Park, White Sands Nat. Mon., El Paso, and Juárez, Mex.

Three days: Tombstone; Tucson; Saguaro, Tumacacori, Chiricahua, and Tonto Nat. Mons.; Phoenix; Organ Pipe Cactus Nat. Mon. Then northwestward—

Two days: To Death Valley Nat. Mon., Las Vegas, Lake Mead, and Hoover Dam.

Two days: To Grand Canyon. Visit both rims if you have time.

Three days: Via Pipe Spring Nat. Mon. and Utah's Dixie to Zion and Bryce Canyons and Cedar Breaks Nat. Mon. Try the dirt road over Boulder Mountain and Capitol Reef Nat. Mon. to Natural Bridges and Arches Nat. Mons. Thence to—

Two days: Grand Junction, Colorado Nat. Mon., Black Canyon of the Gunnison, and via Ouray and Silverton (Million Dollar Highway) to Mesa Verde Nat. Park.

Three days: Either through Monument Valley or through the gas and oil country of NW New Mex. to the Indian (Navajo and Hopi) reservations of NE Arizona, Petrified Forest, and Gallup.

Three days: East on U.S. 66 to the Rio Grande Valley of N New Mex., including Albuquerque, Santa Fe, Taos, and the Indian pueblos and picturesque Spanish-American villages and farms.

ADMISSION AND GUIDE FEES are charged by private and, in some cases, federal and state organizations. Religious agencies may invite offerings. Some national parks and monuments charge fees. Most Indian pueblos charge no visiting fee; some do if pictures are taken.

INDIANS OF THE SOUTHWEST

Familiar Picture—
Navajo and Burro

Man originated in Asia and probably came to North America over a Bering Strait land bridge in many distinct migrations. Some of the migrants, settling in the Southwest, took up life in caves and hunted animals 25,000 or more years ago. By 10,000 years ago, several distinct groups had come or developed; some were hunters, some primitive farmers. Very little is known of man in the Southwest before the beginning of the Christian era. But people living soon after that left their skeletons, tools, and craft work in graves and trash heaps. Study of these remains and dating of them by tree rings and radioactive carbon have enabled scientists to trace several early cultures down to modern Indian groups.

Coronado's arrival in 1540 opened the historic period of Southwestern Indian life and began the long conflict which finally placed Indian tribes on reservations. Today, these picturesque people are citizens. They are being encouraged to expand their colorful arts, customs, and ceremonies and, at the same time, to find a place in today's economy so that they may raise their living standards and have a fair share of opportunity in the Atomic Age.

For more about Indians, read:

PREHISTORIC INDIANS OF THE SOUTHWEST, Wormington, Bull. No. 7, Colo. Mus. Nat. Hist., Denver, 1947.

SOUTHWESTERN ARCHEOLOGY, McGregor, John Wiley & Sons, N. Y., 1941.

MASKED GODS, Frank Waters, Univ. of N. Mex. Press, Albuquerque 1950.

HERE COME THE NAVAHO, Underhill, U. S. Indian Service, Haskell Inst., Lawrence, Kan., 1953.

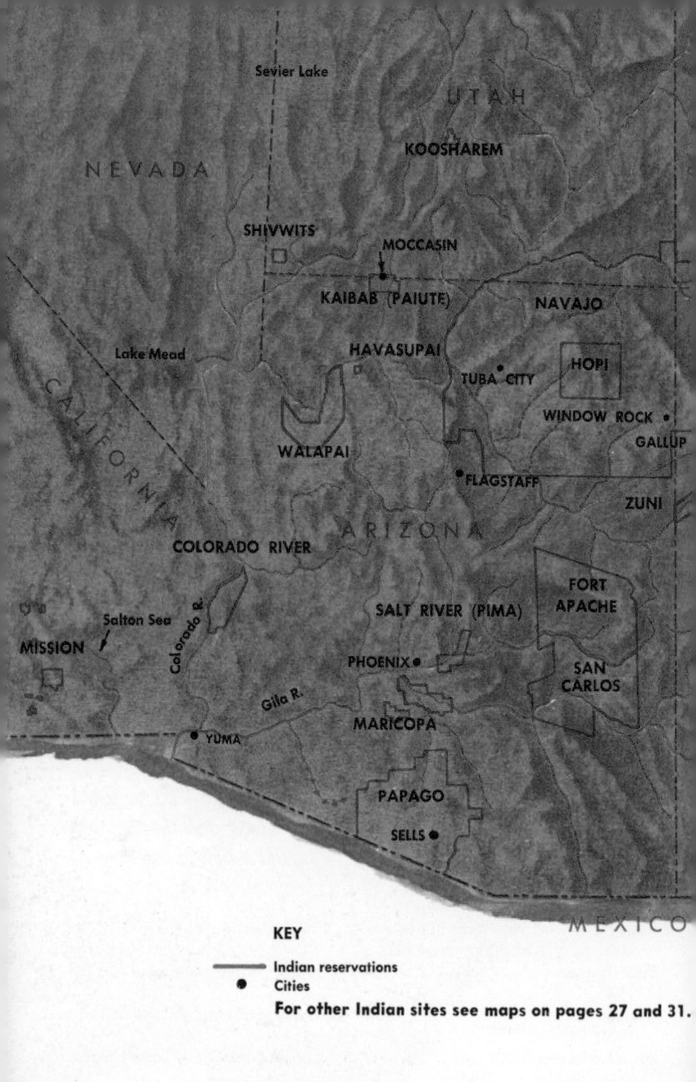

KEY

Indian reservations

Cities

For other Indian sites see maps on pages 27 and 31.

COLORADO

KANSAS

UTE

OKLAHOMA

JICARILLA (APACHE)

TAOS

FORMERLY
INDIAN
TERRITORY

SANTA FE

Canadian R.

RIO GRANDE
PUEBLOS

AMARILLO

ALBUQUERQUE

NEW MEXICO

TEXAS

MESCALERO (APACHE)

EL PASO

Pecos R.

Rio Grande

0 30 60 90 120

One inch equals about 120 miles

EARLIEST INHABITANTS Spear points of flaked stone found with bones of long-extinct bison, camel, mastodon, and mammoth in a cave in the Sandia Mountains near Albuquerque (AL-bu-KER-kee), N. Mex., have been estimated to be 25,000 years old. This earliest record of man in the Southwest has been named the Sandia (san-DEE-ah) Culture. Most famous of the ancient cultures is called Folsom because of finely flaked projectile points found near Folsom, N. Mex., with bones of an extinct bison. Other evidence shows that Folsom people lived between 10,000 and 25,000 years ago. Another group of people, at about the same time, made thick, square-based projectile points, first found near San Jon (HONE), N. Mex. A more recent skeletal discovery of ancient man in western Texas has been named Midland Man.

More recently, people of the Yuma Culture made beautiful, flaked projectile points, first found near Yuma, Colo. Ancient grinding stones found in Ventana Cave, south of Phoenix, Ariz., and also in southwestern New Mexico, mark the Cochise Culture of fruit-and-root-gathering people who lived from 10,000 to 500 B.C. These materials and others found in Gypsum Cave, Nev., and in the Tabeguache Valley of southwestern Colorado are the main records of people in the Southwest before the Christian era.

ANASAZI CULTURE Anasazi (Navajo for "ancient ones") is the name given to the people who lived over all the plateaulands of the northern Southwest in pre-Christian times. Later raiders, disease, or the great drouth (1276-1299 A.D.) forced them to seek new homes, which their descendants, the Pueblo Indians, now occupy. The early Anasazi were called Basketmakers because of basketry remains found in their caves. These people were semi-agricultural; they built slab-lined storage pits, hunted with spear throwers called atlatls, had dogs, wove clothing from skins and plant fibers, and buried food and equipment with their dead to provide for a future life.

By 500-600 A.D. these people had established communities and had learned how to build pithouse shelters. Another important advance was the start of pottery making. Turkeys may have been domesticated during this time. Beans were added to the crops of corn and squash, and the bow and arrow first came into use. By 800 A.D. the beginnings of modern Pueblo Culture were evident.

14th Century Hohokam Watchtower (restored) and Irrigation Canal at Casa Grande National Monument (see p. 136)

HOHOKAM, MOGOLLON, PATAYAN While the Anasazi were laying the foundations of the future Pueblo civilization, several cultures developed in southern deserts and valleys. The Hohokam (ho-ho-KAM, Pima for "those who have gone") were farmers who developed an advanced system of irrigation. Shell jewelry, cremation of the dead, finely woven cotton fabrics, and wattle-and-daub houses marked their culture. Hohokam may have been ancestors of the modern Pimas and Papagos. Less is known of the Mogollon (mogo-YOHN) Culture, which developed (possibly from the earlier Cochise) in the southern New Mexico-Arizona area. Yuman and Patayan (Walapai for "the old people") groups occupied the Colorado River Valley below Grand Canyon. Knowledge of other groups is scant; few remains have been found. While scientists are still searching, visitors should not do unscientific digging and illegal "pothunting" lest evidence be destroyed which is essential in historical research.

RISE OF PUEBLOS Transition, about 700-800 A.D., from Basketmaker to Pueblo is recognized by the development of many-roomed masonry houses and the modification of the old pithouse to a ceremonial chamber or kiva (KEE-vah). Crude stone hoes and axes came into use. Cotton was a new crop, and the loom was developed. The one-story 6- to 14-room houses were built in a double tier or single row, sometimes L- or U-shaped. Pottery developed with variety in form and decoration. Baskets were still made, but pottery took over many uses. New techniques and materials in weaving appeared. The bow and arrow came into general use. Human bodies were buried, in flexed position, in abandoned storage pits or trash heaps, with pottery and other offerings. Anasazi influence spread, evidence of it being found from the Big Bend area in Texas to southeastern Nevada. By 1000 A.D. nearly all Pueblo traits were established and the stage was set for a great Southwest native civilization to burst into bloom.

Typical House—Early Pueblo Period

Cliff Dwellings at Mesa Verde, Colo.

GOLDEN AGE OF PUEBLOS Pueblo Culture reached its peak in the Southwest while the shadow of the Dark Ages lay over Europe. About 1050 A.D. there was a trend toward great, terraced, communal dwellings several stories high, housing hundreds of people. These were built in the open or under protecting cliffs, as at Mesa Verde National Park, Colo. Much local variation in architecture and in the arts and crafts developed. Pottery was made with a richness of form and design. High-quality cotton cloth reflected progress in weaving, and beautiful turquoise jewelry was made. Dry farming, flood-water farming, and irrigation were practiced.

The end of the golden age began before 1300 A.D. Communal dwellings were gradually abandoned until the entire northern area was deserted. No one knows what caused the emigration — perhaps epidemics, attacks by plundering Navajos and Apaches, destruction of farm land by erosion, internal discord, or famine resulting from the great drouth of 1276-1299. At any rate the works of centuries were abandoned and the people moved to places where conditions were more favorable and where we find their descendants today.

ARTS AND CRAFTS OF THE GOLDEN AGE
Arrowheads
Pottery
Turquoise Beads
Tools
Baskets
Rock Pictures

Taos Pueblo

MODERN PUEBLOS After the great communal dwellings were abandoned and new villages established, the rejuvenated Anasazi might have risen to a new cultural peak but for the arrival of Europeans in 1540. The Spanish exploring the Southwest found more than 70 inhabited Indian pueblos (in 1955 there were only 30). After the Spanish came, the Indians absorbed new ideas and adopted new materials including metals and livestock. In 1680 the Pueblos revolted and for 12 years were free of Spanish rule. Even today, after long domination by people of European origin, the Pueblos hold to much of their old way of life. Except for the Zuni and Hopi villages, modern Pueblos are in the Rio Grande or tributary valleys. The Indians farm irrigated lands, raise cattle, or work at a variety of jobs. Government and private agencies stimulate continuation of native arts and crafts, and many products find a tourist market. Dances and ceremonials are still practiced as religious or social observances. Visitors are welcome to the villages and to the public dances.

For more about Pueblo Indians, read NEW MEXICO INDIANS, Bertha P. Dutton, New Mexico Assoc. on Indian Affairs, Santa Fe, N. Mex., 1951, and THE WORKADAY LIFE OF THE PUEBLO INDIANS, Underhill, U.S. Indian Service, Haskell Inst., Lawrence, Kan., 1946.

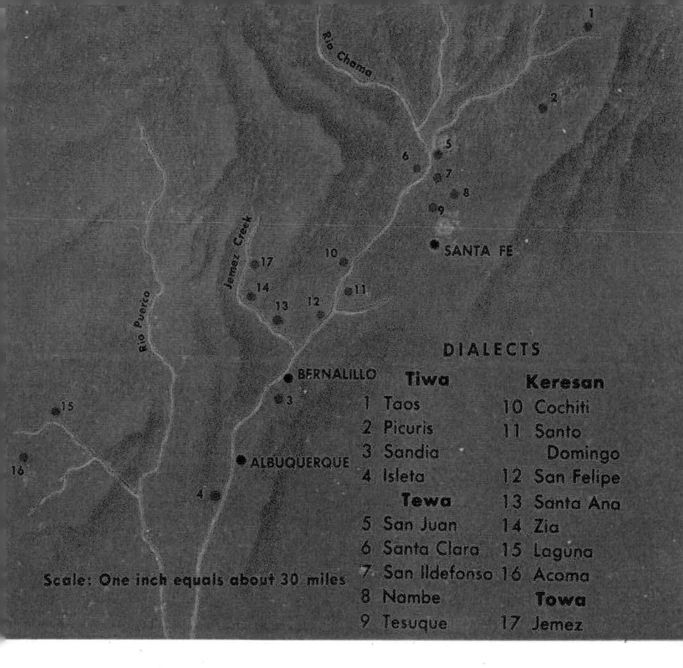

RIO GRANDE PUEBLOS The upper Rio Grande Valley has remains of ancient cultures, modern Indian villages, Spanish-speaking towns, up-to-date cities, and workshops of the atom scientists. Pueblo Indian farmers use modern methods of agriculture, tools, and machinery. The homes of these people are a mixture of the ancient and the modern. They use store clothing for daily wear, but the older women still favor native styles for dress-up occasions. Nominally Christianized, the people retain many religious beliefs of their forefathers. Each family has its ceremonial costumes or has custody of communal religious regalia, which is a cherished responsibility. Many Pueblo Indians speak three languages: their own tribal dialect (noted above), Spanish, and English.

Taos War Dance

PUEBLO DAILY LIFE Although the pueblos are generally alike, each has its own social organization. Secular authority rests in an annually elected governor. Religious activities are controlled by a *cacique* (kah-SEE-kee), who holds office for life. *Principáles* integrate civil and religious matters. Religion, based on the idea that man must live in harmony with nature, transcends all else. It integrates arts, crafts, farming, hunting, and social affairs, and underlies Pueblo legend, poetry, song, ceremony, and dance.

Socially, the people of a pueblo belong to one of two kinship groups, each having several kiva or "church" societies. There is also a kachina, or rain-making, cult. A few pueblos do not permit outsiders to view their masked dances, which are often the final and public performances of sacred rites that have been going on for days. If you are able to see a dance, do not take photographs or make sketches or notes unless you have the specific permission of the pueblo governor. Each pueblo holds a fiesta at a fixed date in honor of its patron saint—a Spanish custom. Early priests gave the name of an appropriate saint to each native ceremonial, to direct the rite into reverence for a Catholic patron. (See p. 13.)

Eagle Dancer

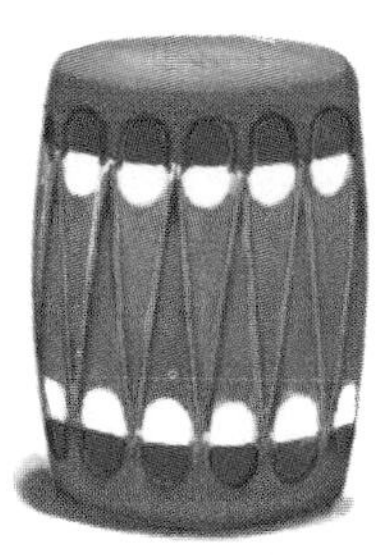

Drum

Pottery

Ceremonial Moccasins and Leggings

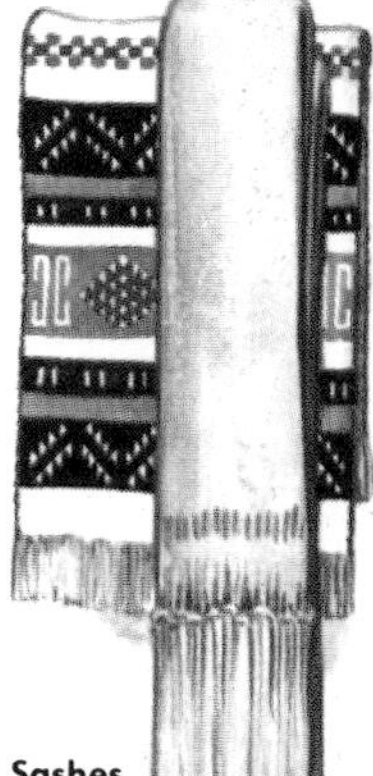

Ceremonial Sashes and Kilts

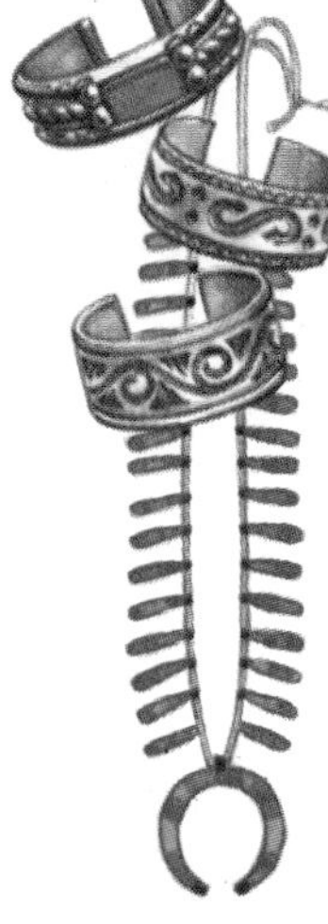

Bracelets and Necklace

Baskets

MODERN RIO GRANDE PUEBLO CRAFT WORK

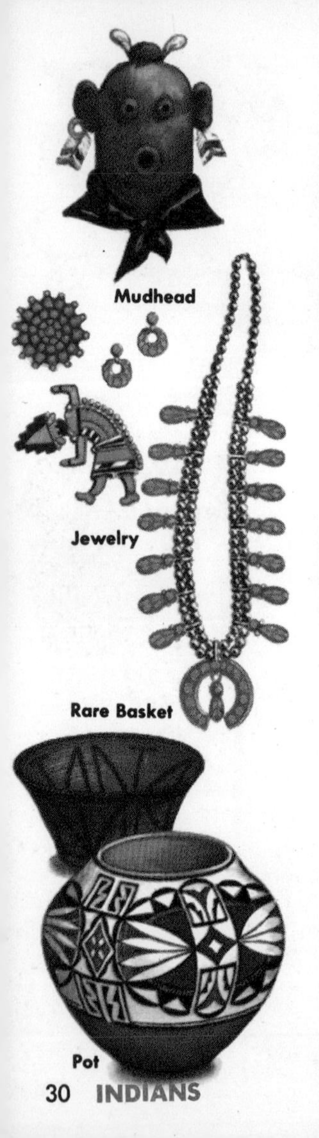
Mudhead
Jewelry
Rare Basket
Pot

THE ZUNIS Thirty-two miles south of Gallup in the largest pueblo in New Mexico live the Zuni (ZOO-nee) people. Of the 20 known village sites, only 7 were inhabited in 1539, when Estevan-the-Moor became the first European to find and be killed by Puebloans. The next year Coronado captured the Zuni village of Hawiku, but, finding no gold, he continued eastward. After 1706 only one Zuni village was occupied. 3 Zuni villages remained.

Zunis are farmers noted for their pottery and turquoise inlay jewelry. From Europeans they learned to work iron, turning to brass and copper about 1840-1850. By 1870 they had adopted silversmithing and had learned the use of stamps and dies from Navajos. About 1890 they began to develop original techniques that led to exquisite inlay work, which they have been doing ever since. The famous Zuni Shalako ceremony held in November or December each year has become a gathering point for students, visitors, and friends of the Indians of all the Southwest.

Hopi Silver Belt

THE HOPIS On the three Hopi (HO-pee) mesas, at the heart of the Navajo Reservation, are nine villages, discovered by Cárdenas (one of Coronado's lieutenants) in 1540. Oraibi is probably one of the two oldest continuously occupied towns in the United States (Acoma, p. 139, is the other). The Hopis though friendly have long resisted European domination. The Spanish tried to convert them, but in 1680 the Hopis uprose with other Pueblo groups, killed the priests, and destroyed the missions. They were never reconquered. Hopi civil officials are also religious leaders. The household centers around the mother and is the pivot of the village religious and social life. The Hopi seek bountiful crops through intricate ceremonies. Snake dances, held each August as a plea for rain, attract hundreds of visitors. Hopi women make beautiful pottery and baskets. Men carve kachina dolls and weave ceremonial garments.

First Mesa	Second Mesa	Third Mesa
1 Walpi	4 Mishongnovi	7 Oraibi
2 Sichomovi	5 Shipaulovi	8 Hotevilla
3 Hano	6 Shungopovi	9 Bacabi

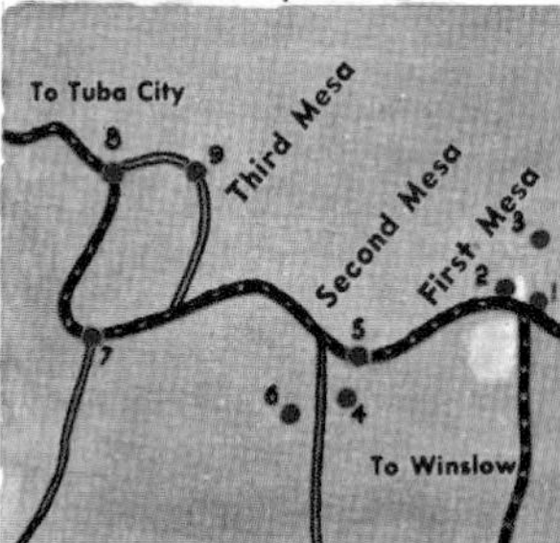

YUMAS AND PAIUTES About 14 Yuman tribes called Rancheria (farmer) Indians occupy the lower Colorado River Valley, the hottest part of the Southwest. Besides farming, they hunt, fish, gather wild fruits, and raise cattle. Northernmost of this group, the Paiutes, or Digger Indians, live where Utah, Nevada, and Arizona meet and in nearby California. The Havasupais, living in a canyon that leads into Grand Canyon, and the Walapai, their neighbors to the west, farm and raise cattle. Below Needles, Calif., are the Chemehuevis, who, like the Cocopahs near Yuma, are indifferent agriculturists. Mohaves, in the early days, sometimes settled group differences in individual combat with clubs of mesquite wood. Yumas and Mohaves constantly resisted newcomers of European origin. Many of the Yuman tribes grew native cotton, which women spun and men wove into cloth.

Yuman Woman Spinning

Harvesting Saguaro Fruit

PIMAS AND PAPAGOS Papagos (Desert People) and Pimas (River People) are related tribes of northern Mexico and southern Arizona. Both are farmers, augmenting their crops with cactus fruits, seeds of mesquite and other wild plants, native vegetables, and wild game. Modern Pimas have added wheat and alfalfa to their ancient crops of corn, beans, squash, cotton, and tobacco. Lacking irrigation water, Papagos raise cattle and depend heavily upon native food plants, such as the fruits of the Giant Cactus, the harvest season for which sets the tribal new year. People of both tribes live in small villages (see p. 139). They were friendly to the early Spanish and other settlers, serving as scouts in the Apache campaigns. Both tribes once made pottery for home use, now make beautiful baskets for the tourist trade.

THE UTES, most warlike tribe on the Colorado-Utah plateau, were little known before Escalante's journey through their territory in 1776. The Utes raided pueblos and Spanish settlements until Chief Ouray (yoo-RAY) made peace in 1879. Recent gas and oil developments on their lands have given the Utes new wealth.

THE KIOWAS, now settled in western Oklahoma, once were among the most feared Plains Indians. Joining forces with the Comanches in 1790, they together fought the invaders of their hunting grounds until forced to sign a treaty (later broken) with the United States in 1865.

THE COMANCHES, lords of the southern plains, ranged east of the Rockies and west to the Rio Grande. They fought the Apaches and traded with the Puebloans. These most skillful of Indian horsemen alternated buffalo hunts with raids into Mexico and attacks on wagon trains traveling the Santa Fe Trail. They were suppressed in 1875.

Kiowa Raiding Party

Apache
Fire Dance

THE APACHES Apaches are believed to have drifted south from northwestern Canada about 1200-1400 A.D. They were hunters and plant gatherers until the acquisition of Spanish horses remade their way of life. The Apaches hunted buffalo, fought the Comanches (who defeated them in 1723), and raided the pueblos. A scourge to travelers, desert farmer Indians, and Spanish settlements for nearly two centuries, they were finally subdued by the United States Army. Geronimo (her-ON-e-moh) and his band were the last to surrender, in 1886. Now the Apaches, of which there are several tribal groups, are excellent stockmen. Their rituals have never been much publicized, the best known being the annual Gahan Ceremonial at Mescalero, N. Mex., July 1-4. The Apache Fire Dance and the Devil Dance are among the spectacular presentations each August at the Inter-Tribal Ceremonial at Gallup, N. Mex.

Navajo Sand Painting

THE NAVAJOS The 70,000 Navajos, on their 24,000-square-mile reservation in Arizona, New Mexico, and Utah, form the largest Indian tribe in the U.S. Their forebears drifted down from Northwest Canada about 1200-1400 A.D. First called Apaches by the Spanish, later designated *Apaches de Nabahu'u* (enemies from farmed lands), they finally became known as Navajos. Wandering hunters and plant gatherers, Navajos preferred to raid the fields of the Pueblos. When, in 1848, the United States obtained the Southwest from Mexico, Kit Carson was commissioned to subdue the Navajos. After destroying their sheep and crops, he rounded up 8,000 of the people and in 1864 moved them to Fort Sumner, N. Mex., as prisoners of war. In 1868 the Navajos signed a peace treaty and returned home. Within 10 years they were established again, and by 1934 their sheep and horses had overgrazed the entire reservation and the people were threatened with famine. Now, with the help of oil and uranium royalties, schools, and irrigated farms, the Navajo leaders are working out a tribal program to make their people self-sufficient.

NAVAJO ARTS AND CUSTOMS Returning from Fort Sumner in 1868, some Navajos undertook farming, but most raised sheep. Flocks and crops are owned by women. The wife is the center of the family; the children are hers and members of her clan. Women and children herd and butcher the sheep, spin the wool, and weave rugs, which are exchanged for clothing, coffee, sugar, or canned foods. Women and children still dress in 1860 styles, wearing long, full, calico skirts and colorful velveteen blouses. Men retain their pride in horsemanship and their wealth in horses. Many men now work for wages. Previously, silversmithing was important men's work. With crude tools and silver dollars or Mexican pesos, Navajo men developed the heavy silver jewelry for which the tribe is famous. Now they use silver slugs or wire to make rings, bracelets, pins, buckles, necklaces, and concho belts. Men represent their families at ceremonies and in public. All rituals have a definite objective: to secure food, insure survival, regain health, or cast out evil spirits. These rites, called "sings," are important also as social gatherings.

Navajo Silversmith

Navajo Loom and Hogan

NAVAJO WEAVING Navajo families in winter live in dome-shaped hogans made of logs or stones and earth. In summer, when they are on the move searching for grass for the sheep, they build a simple brush shelter wherever they stay for a few days. Here the wife does housekeeping and sets up her loom, weaving rugs when time permits. All members of the family help with shearing, but the children watch the sheep and the women wash, card, spin, and dye the wool. Navajos learned weaving from the Pueblos and, soon after obtaining sheep from the Spanish, began weaving blankets, using their own wool and native dyes. With twisted yarns and commercial dyes, new designs came. Navajos prefer lighter, more colorful Pendleton wool blankets; so, after 1890, they began to make rugs for sale. In recent years weaving has declined.

For more about Navajos and Apaches read:

TRADERS TO THE NAVAHO, Wetherill, Univ. of N. Mex. Press, Albuquerque, 1952.

APACHE AGENT, Clum, Houghton Mifflin Co., Boston, 1936.

NAVAHO SHEPHERD AND WEAVER, Gladys Amanda Reichard, J. J. Augustin, Locust Valley, L. I., N. Y., 1936.

APACHE DAYS AND AFTER, Criese, Caxton Printers, Caldwell, Ida., 1941.

NAVAHO WEAVING, Amsden, Univ. of N. Mex. Press, Albuquerque, 1949.

THE NAVAHO, Kluckhohn and Leighton, Harvard Univ. Press, Cambridge, Mass., 1947.

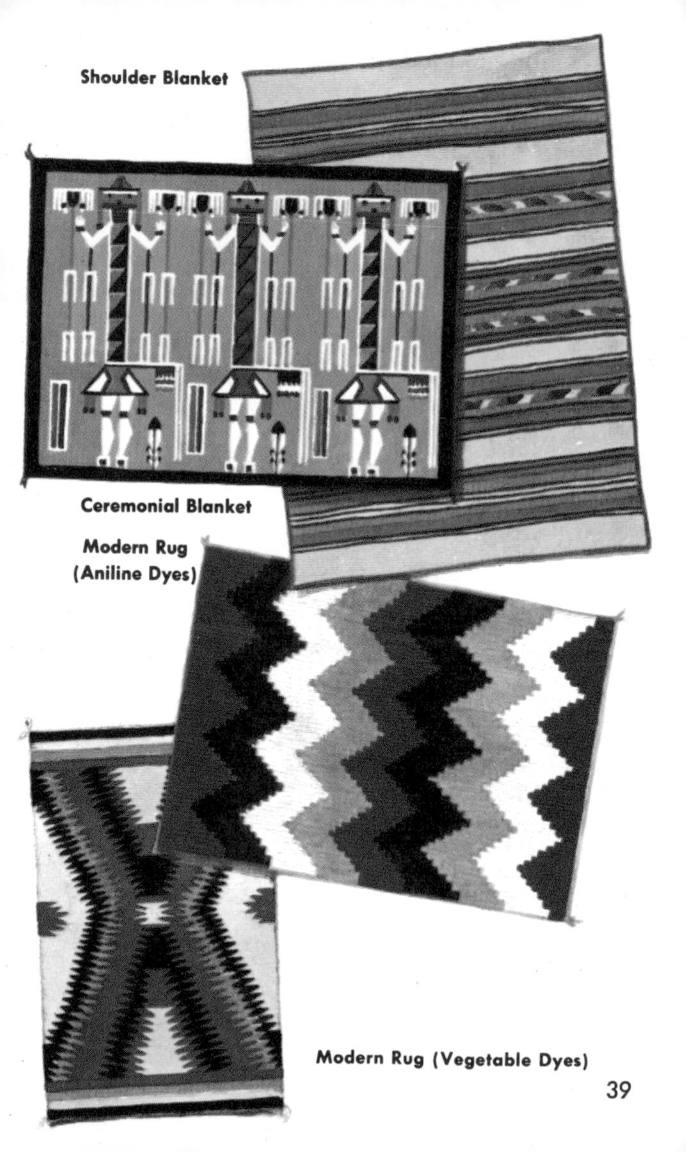

Shoulder Blanket

Ceremonial Blanket

Modern Rug (Aniline Dyes)

Modern Rug (Vegetable Dyes)

HISTORICAL TIMETABLE

1276-99: Long drouth forces Indians to seek new homes.
1536: Cabeza de Vaca crosses Southwest en route to New Spain.
1540-42: Coronado explores Southwest from Grand Canyon to Kansas.
1581-1600: Many Spanish expeditions follow Coronado.
1598: Juan de Oñate sets up first capital at San Juan.
1610: New capital at Santa Fe, terminus of Mexican route.
1680: Pueblo Indians revolt and drive out Spanish.
1692: De Vargas recaptures SW. Father Kino develops chain of missions among Pima and Papago Indians.
1776: Escalante explores present W Colorado and Utah.
1803: Louisiana Purchase brings United States into SW.
1813: Old Spanish Trail partly follows Escalante's route.
1822: Mexico wins independence from Spain.
1824: U.S. trappers push into SW from east and north.
1830-31: Old Spanish Trail extended to California.
1833: Vein gold discovered in New Mexico.
1844: Fremont explores Utah and Colorado until 1853.
1846: Texas joins U.S. as 28th state. War with Mexico!
1847: Mormons settle Utah and open wagon route from Santa Fe to California.

1848: Mexican War ends. SW transferred to U.S. with boundary along Rio Grande and Gila River.

1849: Stages begin operation over the Santa Fe Trail. Gold rush brings deaths along Camino del Diablo.

1850: U.S. buys "Santa Fe County" from Texas.

1853: Gadsden Purchase sets final Mexican boundary.

1854-56: Silver mining reaches a new high in Arizona.

1857-59: Beale through SW with camels. Pikes Peak gold rush.

1862: Civil War splits SW. Texans invade New Mexico.

1860-1890: Mormons from Utah colonize Arizona.

1864: Navajos defeated by Kit Carson, moved to Ft. Sumner.

1866: Nevada joins Union as 36th state.

1869: Powell's boats conquer Colorado River in Grand Canyon.

1873: Crook subdues Tontos, Yavapaís and Walapais.

1876: Coal mining started in Utah. Barbed wire ends epoch of open range. Colorado becomes 38th state.

1877-78: Tombstone and Bisbee—mining boom towns.

1881: SW connected to Pacific Coast by railroad.

1886: Geronimo surrenders, ending Indian resistance.

1896: Utah becomes 45th state.

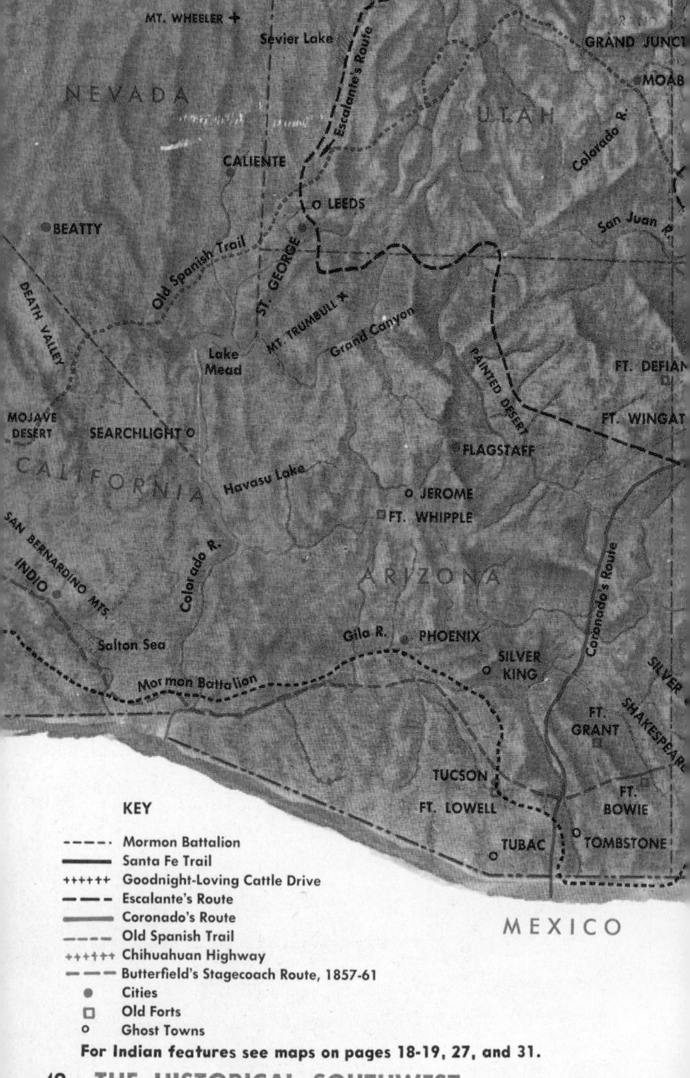
MT. WHEELER
Sevier Lake
Escalante's Route
GRAND JUNCT
MOAB
NEVADA
UTAH
Colorado R.
CALIENTE
LEEDS
BEATTY
Old Spanish Trail
ST. GEORGE
San Juan R.
DEATH VALLEY
MT. TRUMBULL
Grand Canyon
Lake Mead
PAINTED DESERT
FT. DEFIAN
MOJAVE DESERT
SEARCHLIGHT
FT. WINGAT
FLAGSTAFF
CALIFORNIA
Havasu Lake
JEROME
FT. WHIPPLE
SAN BERNARDINO MTS.
INDIO
Colorado R.
ARIZONA
Coronado's Route
Salton Sea
Gila R.
PHOENIX
SILVER KING
SILVER
Mormon Battalion
FT. GRANT
SHAKESPEARE
TUCSON
FT. LOWELL
FT. BOWIE
TUBAC
TOMBSTONE
MEXICO
KEY
Mormon Battalion
Santa Fe Trail
Goodnight-Loving Cattle Drive
Escalante's Route
Coronado's Route
Old Spanish Trail
Chihuahuan Highway
Butterfield's Stagecoach Route, 1857-61
Cities
Old Forts
Ghost Towns
For Indian features see maps on pages 18-19, 27, and 31.

MT. MASSIVE
MT. ELBERT
PIKES PEAK
FT. WALLACE
KANSAS
COLORADO
PUEBLO
Goodnight-Loving Cattle Drive
FT. GARLAND
Santa Fe Trail
BENT'S FORT
Arkansas R.
FT. DODGE
RTON
CREEDE
SAN JUAN MTS.
ALAMOSA
Cimarron Cut-off on Santa Fe Trail
Cimarron R.
d Spanish Trail
Rio Grande
OKLAHOMA
TAOS
Escalante's Route
FT. MARCY
SANTA FE
FT. UNION
Coronado's Route
Canadian R.
AMARILLO
GOLDEN
BUQUERQUE
Coronado's Route
Prairie Dog Town Fork
FT. SUMNER
EW MEXICO
FT. CRAIG
Brazos R.
LUBBOCK
FT. STANTON
Chihuahuan Highway
LAVA BEDS
SACRAMENTO MTS.
Pecos R.
TEXAS
CARLSBAD
FT. CUMMINGS
FT. BLISS
EL PASO
Butterfield's Route
FT. STOCKTON
FT. DAVIS
Rio Grande
ALPINE
Pecos R.
SANTIAGO MTS.
0 30 60 90 120
TERLINGUA
One inch equals about 120 miles

THE MODERN SOUTHWEST

Continuous development has occurred since 1900. Climate has been vital in attracting tourists and various military establishments. Huge dams and deep wells have brought water to stimulate progress.

1903: Three great natural bridges found in SE Utah.

1906: Act for Preservation of American Antiquities sets base for national monuments, archeological research.

1908: Grand Canyon made National Monument. Became Park in 1919.

1910: Roosevelt Dam completion opens irrigation era.

1912: New Mexico and Arizona become states.

1918: Logging industry enters boom period in SW.

1923: New Mexico floods show need for prevention.

1924: Carlsbad Caverns made National Monument. Became Park in 1930.

1929: Piping natural gas brings this fuel into wider use.

1934: Indian Reorganization Act provides self-rule.

1935: Deep wells stimulate agricultural development.

1936: Hoover Dam completed.

1938: "Dust Bowl" in W Texas and Oklahoma arouses SW.

1940: Coronado Cuarto Centennial observed. Santa Gertrudis breed of cattle developed.

1945: Atomic Era opened by explosion of test bomb.

1947: Rocket testing begins at White Sands.

1948: Uranium discoveries open SW "back country."

1953: Pipe-line projects expand natural-gas industry.

1954: U.S. Air Force Academy set up at Colorado Springs. Human skeletal remains, oldest known in U.S., discovered at Midland, Tex.

SOME IMPORTANT CITIES

Southwestern Kansas

Liberal: Natural gas center. Gateway to sand hills and Meade State Park.

Garden City: Near Buffalo, Point-Rocks, Scott, Finney, Hodgeman State Parks.

Dodge City: Center of wheat, shortgrass belt. Ft. Dodge and Beeson Museum.

Western Oklahoma

Freedom: Crystal Caverns, Little Salt Plain, Cedar Canyon Park.

Kenton: Gateway to Black Mesa, Dinosaur Quarry, Hallock Park.

Altus: Near Washita Mts. Nat. Wildlife Ref. Reserve and Quartz Mt.

Western Texas

Amarillo: Center of wheat and cattle country, site of government helium plant, gateway to Palo Duro State Park and Plains Historical Museum at Canyon, Tex.

Lubbock: Oil fields, MacKenzie and Big Spring State Parks.

San Angelo: Center of cattle, sheep, and goat industry; Ft. Concho State Park and Museum. On route of early stagecoach lines and cattle drive trails.

Alpine: Gateway to Rio Grande area, Big Bend Nat. Park, and Davis Mt. State Park. Cattle and antelope country.

El Paso: Ft. Bliss and Biggs Field. Rich farming area. Carlsbad Caverns, White Sands Nat. Mon., Cloudcroft recreation area in N. Mex., and (through Juárez) Mex.

Southern Colorado

Colorado Springs: U.S. Air Force Academy. Annual rodeo. Taylor Museum Fine Arts Center. Gateway to Garden of Gods, Manitou Springs, and Pikes Peak.

Pueblo: Huge steel mills and Helen Hunt Jackson house. Near farm and cattle country, Spanish Peaks hunting and fishing areas.

Salida: Center of routes into majestic Continental Divide country. Royal Gorge and Arkansas River scenery and fishing.

Alamosa: Center of rich San Luis Valley farming area. Gateway to southern Rockies, Great Sand Dunes Nat. Mon., Ft. Garland, Taos and Eagle Nest Lake, N.M.

Durango: Center of last (D&RGW) narrow-gage railroad. Gateway to Silverton-Ouray mining districts and south end of Million Dollar Highway. Jump-off for hunting-fishing trips into San Juan and La Plata Mountains.

Grand Junction: Junction of the Colorado and Gunnison. Grand Valley orchards. Grand Mesa, Black Canyon of Gunnison Nat. Mon., Chipeta State Park, fishing.

New Mexico

Raton: Center of coal and cattle country; gateway to Capulin Mountain Nat. Mon., prehistoric Folsom man quarry, Philmont Boy Scout Camp, Vermejo Park, and hunting and fishing country of the Sangre de Cristo Mountains.

Santa Fe (see p. 144): Home of the State Museum and others, U.S. Indian School, and famous art colony. State capital. Gateway to Hyde State Park, Aspen Basin Ski Area, Indian pueblos, Spanish-American towns, and hunting and fishing in the Sangre de Cristo Mountains.

Albuquerque: Home of University of New Mexico, Kirtland Field, and Sandia Secret Weapons Base; gateway to La Madera Ski Area and Indian pueblos.

Gallup: Site of annual mid-August Indian ceremonials. Gateway to Navajo Indian Reservation, Zuni Pueblo, El Morro and Chaco Canyon Nat. Mons., Mt. Taylor volcanic field, Zuni Mountains, and "Four Corners" country.

Roswell: Airbase city among cotton farms. Gateway to Bottomless Lakes State Park, Sacramento and Capitan Mountains, Apache Indian Reservation, Cloudcroft, Ruidoso, and Lincoln County of Billy-the-Kid fame.

Carlsbad: Near nation's largest potash mines, oil fields, Pecos farm and cattle country. Gateway to Carlsbad Caverns Nat. Park.

Silver City: Gateway to Santa Rosa open-pit copper mine, Gila Wilderness Area, Mogollon Mountains, Black Range, and Gila Cliff Dwellings Nat. Mon.

Arizona

Douglas: Site of giant smelters. Gateway to Bisbee mines, Old Tombstone, Chiricahua Nat. Mon., and (through Agua Prieta) to Mexico.

Tucson (TOO-sahn): Home of state university and museum, Davis—Monthan Airbase. Gateway to cattle country; Arizona-Sonora Desert Museum; Papago Indian Reservation; San Xavier Mission; Colossal Cave; Tumacacori, Saguaro, and Organ Pipe Cactus Nat. Mons. From Tucson you go through Nogales (by road or rail) into Mexico.

Phoenix: State capital, site of Pueblo Grande Ruins and Heard and Arizona Museums; center of citrus fruit industry and rich vegetable, cotton, and cattle-feeding croplands. Gateway to the Arizona desert, Salt River power projects, dude ranches, Gulf of California fishing, Pima and Papago Indian Reservations, Tonto and Casa Grande Nat. Mons.

Huge Irrigation Systems Water Millions of Acres

Globe: Center, with Miami, of copper mining and smelting; S. W. Archeological Center; Besh-bagowa Ruin; gateway to Apache Indian Reservation, Superior Mines, Boyce-Thompson Arboretum, and White Mountain fishing.

Prescott: Site of Old Ft. Whipple; gateway to Joshua Tree forest, Jerome (ghost town), Verde Valley, Tuzigoot, and Montezuma Castle Nat. Mons.

Winslow: Gateway to Navajo and Hopi Reservations, Meteor Crater, Painted Desert, Petrified Forest Nat. Mon., and State Antelope-Buffalo Reserve.

Flagstaff: Center of sawmill industry; site of Lowell Observatory, Museum of Northern Arizona, and July 4 Indian Pow-Wow. Gateway to Grand Canyon, and to Walnut Canyon, Sunset Crater, and Wupatki Nat. Mons. Take-off point for Navajo and Hopi Indian Reservations, Monument Valley, Oak Creek Canyon, San Francisco Peaks, hunting and fishing of N. Arizona, and Navajo and Rainbow Bridge Nat. Mons.

Southern Utah

Cedar City: Gateway to Utah's Dixie; "Arizona Strip"; Zion and Bryce Canyon Nat. Parks; Cedar Breaks, Pipe Spring, and Grand Canyon Nat. Mon.

Fillmore: Site of Old Statehouse State Park; gateway to Escalante Wilderness and hunting and fishing areas of Aquarius Plateau.

Green River: Gateway to Coldwater Geyser, uranium mines, Capitol Reef and Arches Nat. Mons.; jump-off for Colorado River boat trips.

Southeastern Nevada

Ely: In famous mining district; gateway to Paiute Indian Res., Lehman Caves Nat. Mon., Snake Mt. hunting area, and proposed Great Basin Nat. Park.

Las Vegas: Site of Pioneer Village Museum and Nellis Field Trainer Base; gateway to Hoover Dam, Valley of Fire, and Lakes Mead and Mohave.

Beatty: Site of old mining district, Bottle House Museum; gateway to ghost towns, Desert Wildlife Refuge, and Death Valley Nat. Mon.

Southwestern California

El Centro: With Brawley, center of Imperial Valley farming area and gateway to Mexicali, Mexico, and weird desert of Salton Sea.

Palm Springs: Spa for Hollywood notables; with Indio, gateway to Joshua Tree Nat. Mon. and south entrance of Death Valley.

Sky Harbor, Phoenix, Ariz.

MODERN LIFE AND INDUSTRIES Today's Southwest is a land of contrasts. Atom scientists from new, ultra-modern Los Alamos en route to Spanish-speaking Santa Fe (oldest capital city in the United States) pass Indian pueblos where potters use methods a thousand years old. Travelers in Diesel-drawn Pullmans flash past burros laden with wood for cooking fires. Armies of hunters, skiers, fishermen, "rockhounds," photographers, and sightseers invade this land each year to enjoy the scenery, climate, and their hobbies. They help build the Southwest's booming tourist industry.

Huge irrigation systems water millions of acres of cotton, citrus, alfalfa, apple, peach, corn, wheat, and other crops. From desert cattle tanks to the droning generators of Hoover Dam, the Southwest's first caution is "Go easy with water!" Here is a sun-warmed land of modern cities and wide ranges; of forested mountains and cactus-studded deserts; of rich farms and rocky mesas where coal, gold, lead, pumice, and copper are mined and where prospectors search for still-hidden uranium, petroleum, and other earth treasures. The figures on p. 49 give a general picture of recent Southwestern production and progress.

THE MODERN SOUTHWEST—RESOURCES AND OTHER STATISTICS

(Acres, K.W.H., and dollars are in millions; values are annual)

	ARIZONA	NEW MEXICO	UTAH	COLORADO	TEXAS	NEVADA
Area (in sq. miles)	114,000	122,000	85,000	104,000	267,000	111,000
Population, 1950	750,000	681,000	689,000	1,325,000	7,711,000	160,000
Capital city	Phoenix	Santa Fe	Salt Lake City	Denver	Austin	Carson City
Acres natl. forests	12.2	10.3	9.1	15.2	1.7	5.4
Livestock values	$ 95.7	$107.5	$112.6	$323.9	$ 848.3	$32.0
Farm crop values	$276.0	$195.4	$ 38.4	$558.1	$1,147.4	$16.0
Oil and gas values	—	$161.6	$ 3.2	$ 97.3	$2,362.6	—
Mineral values	$181.1	$199.6	$177.7	$228.5	$2,365.8	$37.4
Farm land acreage	37.9	49.6	10.3	36.2	141.3	6.2
Acres irrigated	1.4	0.7	1.1	2.9	2.7	0.7
Tourist values	$200	$175	$ 31.7	$265.3	$ 770.5	—
Mfg. prod. values	$104	$55.5	$128.3	$286.8	$1,727.5	$27.8
K.W.H. (kilowatt-hours) produced	3,770	1,820	2,700	2,260	7,280	—
Nat. parks and mons.	17	9	11	8	1	2
State parks and mons.	0	15	6	0	48	11

PLANTS AND ANIMALS In traveling notice abrupt changes in vegetation. A pinyon-juniper forest gives place to grassland studded with yuccas; Creosotebush and Saltbush merge into cactus, Mesquite, and Palo-Verde. The group of plant species normally found growing together in a common environment is called a "plant association." Animal species, including insects, prefer particular plant associations for food and shelter, so each vegetative type becomes part of a "community" of plants and animals. Elevation, soil, and other factors determine the nature of communities. Where moisture is all-important, plant associations show seasonal changes. Some species live through long dry periods in the seed stage; others become dormant; still others develop water-storage organs or other devices enabling them to remain active through drouth. Species unable to endure extreme conditions are replaced

LIFE ZONE	ELEVATIONS, feet above sea level (approx.)	TYPE OF COUNTRY	RAINFALL, inches per year
Arctic-alpine	Above 12,000	Above timberline	30-35
Hudsonian	9,500-12,000	High mountains to timberline	30-35
Canadian	8,000-10,000	Mountains	25-30
Transition	7,000-8,000	Plateaulands	19-25
Upper Sonoran	3,500-7,000	Mesas and foothills	12-20
Lower Sonoran	500-4,000	Sonoran, Mohave and Chihuahuan deserts	3-15
Dry-tropical	Below 500	Along Colorado River in extreme SW Arizona	1-6

by those that can. If a species thrives abnormally, its predators act to control it. The natural system of controls is called a "biological balance." Activities of man sometimes upset it and give certain species an advantage. Each Southwest association or community is restricted to specific elevational belts, or zones, above or below which climatic conditions are unfavorable to it.

Life Zones As you go from the desert up to the mesas and on into the mountains, you notice falling temperature, increased moisture, and marked differences in the plant and animal life. The great naturalist C. Hart Merriam showed that such changes due to elevation resemble those due to latitude. Roughly, a change in elevation of 1,000 ft. equals a north-south difference of 300 miles. This theory helps explain the Southwest's complex plant life and animals dependent upon it.

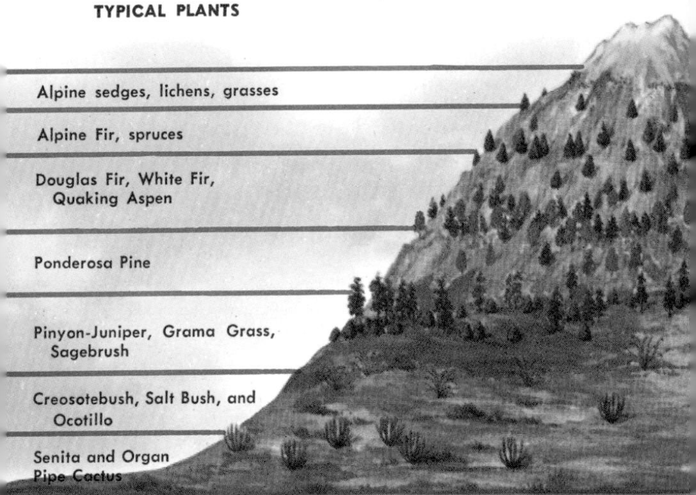

(Table from *Southwest Trees*, U.S. Dept. of Agriculture, 1950.)

PLANT GEOGRAPHY Each life zone (pp. 50-51) is represented—arctic and dry-tropical rarely. Most peaks above timberline are accessible only by foot or horseback. The Pikes Peak summit road goes into the arctic-alpine life zone. Hudsonian plant communities occur along highways through some mountain passes. Canadian life zone plants appear along mountain roads in New Mexico, Colorado, Arizona, Utah, and Nevada. Ponderosa Pine, chief Southwest lumber tree, indicates transition life-zone conditions wherever it grows abundantly.

Arctic-Alpine Zone
San Francisco Mts., Ariz.
Sangre de Cristo Mts., N. Mex.
San Juan Mts., Colo.
Uncompahgre Mts., Colo.
Snake Range, Nev.
Wasatch Mts., Utah
Pikes Peak, Colo.

Hudsonian Zone
Cedar Breaks Nat. Mon., Utah
Bryce Canyon, Utah
N. Rim Grand Canyon, Ariz.
Wolf Creek Pass, Colo.
Million Dollar Highway, Colo.
Monarch Pass, Colo.
Lizard Head Pass, Colo.

Canadian Zone
Kaibab Plateau, Ariz.
White Mts., Ariz.
Sandia Mts., N. Mex.
Black Range, N. Mex.
Sacramento Mts., N. Mex.
Aquarius Plateau, Utah
Charleston Mts., Nev.

Transition Zone
Chiricahua Mts., Ariz.
Santa Catalina Mts., Ariz.
Chisos Mts., Tex.
Davis Mts., Tex.
Zuni Mts., N. Mex.
La Sal Mts., Utah
plateaus, SW Utah.

Conditions favorable to upper Sonoran vegetation are more widespread in the Southwest than any other conditions. Mesa lands and foothills covered with pygmy forests of pinyon and juniper are typical. Lower Sonoran conditions prevail across the entire southern portion of the Southwest, reaching north into southeast Nevada and southwest Utah. Although conditions typical of the dry-tropical life zone do not enter the Southwest, comparable vegetation is found along the Colorado River above its delta. It appears, also, from the Gulf of California, along the valley of the Sonoita River, to the southern portion of Organ Pipe Cactus National Monument south of Ajo, Ariz.

BIRDS

Red-tailed Hawk

Birds are seen everywhere in the Southwest from hot, dry deserts to arctic mountain tops. Some species are residents; others migrate through the Southwest. Many of the 400 species recorded in the Southwest are found elsewhere in this country. The following pages deal only with the birds characteristic of the Southwest and common enough to be seen frequently. Since elevation is important in determining local climate and food supply, birds are classified as mountain, mesa, and desert species. However, a species may be found at higher elevations in summer than in winter. Insect eaters are generally absent at high altitudes, where cold limits their food supply. Less active during the heat of the day, birds are best seen in early morning or late afternoon. A slow walk, away from houses, will reveal birds you otherwise would miss, though jays and some others make themselves at home near camps and cabins. All songbirds are protected by federal and state laws.

Common Raven

For more about birds read:

BIRDS, Zim and Gabrielson, Golden Press, N. Y., 1956

BIRDS OF THE WEST, Booth, Stanford Univ. Press, Palo Alto, Calif., 1950

FIELD GUIDE TO THE BIRDS OF TEXAS, Peterson, Texas Game and Fish Commission, 1960

FIELD GUIDE TO WESTERN BIRDS, Peterson, Houghton Mifflin, Boston, 1941

GUIDE TO BIRD FINDING WEST OF THE MISSISSIPPI, Pettingill, Oxford Univ. Press, N. Y., 1953

BIRDS OF THE MOUNTAINS

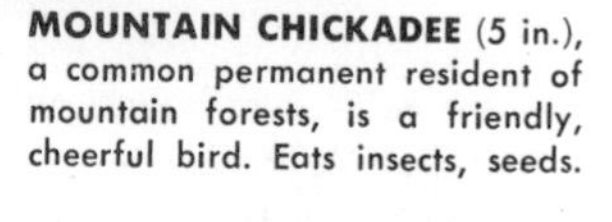

MOUNTAIN CHICKADEE (5 in.), a common permanent resident of mountain forests, is a friendly, cheerful bird. Eats insects, seeds.

HAIRY WOODPECKER (9 in.) is known by the white stripe on its back. Only males have the red head patch. Eats insects.

MOUNTAIN BLUEBIRD (7 in.) is bright blue with a characteristic white belly. It often travels in flocks in winter. The food consists mainly of insects.

CALLIOPE HUMMINGBIRD (3 in.) is the smallest U.S. hummer. It prefers high mountain meadows of lupine and paintbrush in summer.

BLUE GROUSE (21 in.) and the similar but smaller Spruce Grouse live among spruce, fir, and aspens, feeding on leaves and shoots. Food sources are endangered by overgrazing.

DIPPER (7½ in.) lives near swift streams and waterfalls, nesting in moist locations. It seeks aquatic insects under the water.

BROWN-CAPPED FINCH (6 in.) lives in snow above timberline in summer, winters in valleys. Eats insects, seeds. Nests on ground.

WHITE-BREASTED NUTHATCH (6 in.) clings head-down on tree trunks, looking for insects and seeds. It stores food. This bird chatters constantly.

CLARK'S NUTCRACKER (12½ in.) summers in mountain forests. It will enter camps to beg food. In winter it descends to the pines and pinyons.

STELLER'S JAY (13 in.), of Ponderosa Pine country, is handsome and arrogant. Hops about on the ground, hunting food and trouble. Call is loud and harsh.

BIRDS OF THE MESAS

ROCK WREN (5½ in.) is a sprightly, grayish-brown songster of canyon and mesa. Whitish tail patch. Winters in desert valleys.

BLACK-BILLED MAGPIE (20 in.) is a handsome, noisy bird. Colonies nest in trees and thickets, feed on insects, carrion and grain.

MOURNING DOVE (12 in.), brownish, with pointed tail, is common. Nests on ground or low trees. Song is mournful "Coo-ah, coo, coo, coo."

WESTERN MEADOWLARK (9 in.), a chunky, brown and yellow songster of grasslands, has a black V on the breast. It eats seeds and various insects.

GOLDEN EAGLE (35 in.), a bird of mesa and mountain, is larger and darker than hawks. Young have white under wings. Eats rodents, carrion. Bald Eagle is rare in the Southwest.

BIRDS OF THE MESAS

SAY'S PHOEBE (7 in.), a buffy flycatcher with tawny breast, nests in buildings and under ledges. It snaps up insects on the wing.

SCRUB JAY (12 in.) is a crestless, pale blue bird with a streaked gray chest. Noisy. Lives in oak and pinyon-juniper scrub.

PINYON JAY (11 in.) is chunky and dark. Flocks frequent junipers and pinyons. They are frequently seen on the ground.

BROWN TOWHEE (9 in.) is fluffy, brown, sparrow-like. Lives and nests on the ground in brushland. Eats seeds and insects.

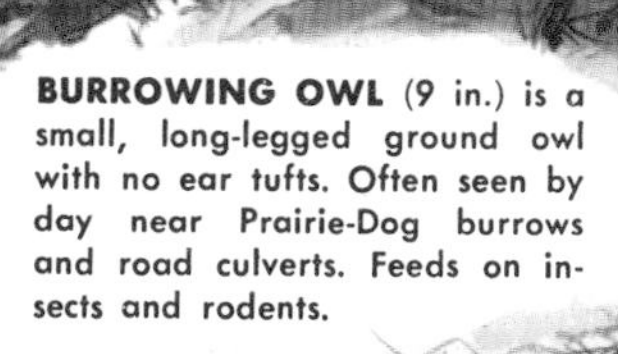

BURROWING OWL (9 in.) is a small, long-legged ground owl with no ear tufts. Often seen by day near Prairie-Dog burrows and road culverts. Feeds on insects and rodents.

BIRDS OF THE DESERT

PHAINOPEPLA (7 in.) is crested, glossy blue-black, with white wing patches in flight, and flute-like song. Eats berries and insects.

CACTUS WREN (7 in.) builds nests for shelter as well as for rearing young, usually in cholla or mesquite. Noisy. Eats insects.

SPARROW HAWK (9½ in.), is a handsome bird, which feeds mainly on grasshoppers and small mammals. It is widespread in the Southwest.

LOGGERHEAD SHRIKE (9 in.) captures grasshoppers, lizards, and small mammals. Impales surplus prey on thorns. Noisy. Bill has hooked tip.

ROADRUNNER (22 in.) state bird of New Mexico, rarely flies unless frightened. Solitary member of the cuckoo family. Eats insects, lizards, snakes. Seen along roadsides and under bushes.

GILA (HE-lah) **WOODPECKER** (9 in.), named for the valley where it is most abundant, nests in cottonwoods or in stems of Giant Cactus.

ASH-THROATED FLYCATCHER (8 in.) frequents thickets where insects abound. Has slender body, large head, and pale yellow belly.

COMMON NIGHTHAWK (9 in.), fills the air in erratic flight during summer dusk and dawn while pursuing insects. Nests on bare ground.

CRISSAL THRASHER (11½ in.) and three more desert thrashers all are rich songsters. They feed on the ground and nest in cactuses.

GAMBEL'S QUAIL (10 in.), a game bird with curved head plume similar to California Quail, has a chestnut crown. Feeds and nests on the ground. Coveys converse in soft, spirited tones.

REPTILES

The reptiles of the Southwest include turtles, lizards, and snakes. The warm, dry climate favors the last two groups. All reptiles are "cold-blooded"; their temperature is about that of their surroundings. Stories as to the danger from desert reptiles are often exaggerated. Caution in walking through brush or climbing rocky places is common sense.

Turtles of the Southwest include both land (tortoises) and water species. Their shells, plated skins, and horny beaks set them off from other reptiles. Look for the famed Desert Tortoise at lower elevations.

Lizards are common throughout the Southwest. Some look like miniature dinosaurs; most eat insects and other small creatures. Only one lizard, the Gila Monster, is poisonous. It should never be handled.

Snakes are colorful and interesting. Many kinds (especially in summer) feed only at night. They eat insects, lizards, and small rodents. Most snakes are beneficial. Of the poisonous species in the Southwest, only rattlers are dangerous. Wear stout shoes when hiking and climbing. Always look before you step.

For further information read:

REPTILES AND AMPHIBIANS, Zim and Smith, Golden Press, N. Y., 1956.
SNAKES ALIVE AND HOW THEY LIVE, Pope, Viking Press, N. Y., 1937.
HANDBOOK OF LIZARDS, Smith, Cornell Univ. Press, Ithaca, N. Y., 1946.
POISONOUS DWELLERS OF THE DESERT, Dodge, Southwestern Monuments Assoc., Globe, Ariz., 1955.

DESERT TORTOISE (10 in.), a heavy, club-footed, plant-eating turtle, can live several weeks without water. Activity governed by temperature. Female buries leathery-skinned eggs in sand to be hatched by sun's heat.

WESTERN BOX TURTLE (5-6 in.) prefers open, moist areas; may be seen along highways. Under-shell is hinged. Box turtles feed on insects and fruits. Fine pets; may live up to 80 years.

SONORAN MUD TURTLE (5 in.), like its eastern relatives, lives in permanent, sluggish streams, lakes, reservoirs. Long, smooth-shelled; emits characteristic musky odor. Feeds on young of aquatic insects.

EMORY'S SOFT-SHELLED TURTLE (18 in.; to 35 lb.) is the only Southwest member of an edible group with long necks and short tempers. Handle with care. Soft-edged shells; lack horny scales. Live in streams, reservoirs, lakes.

MOUNTAIN AND MESA LIZARDS

CLIMBING UTAS (6 in.), alert and agile, inhabit trees, cliffs, and rocky places, where they feed on insects. When quiet, their skin blends with the color of their surroundings.

COLLARED LIZARDS (14 in.) bite readily but are harmless. They inhabit mountain canyons; are fairly common. Run on hind legs when frightened. Eat insects and small lizards.

SHORT-HORNED LIZARD (4 in.), called "Horned Toad," eats ants and other small insects. It is illegal to remove this easily captured lizard from Arizona or New Mexico.

8-LINED WHIPTAIL LIZARD (11 in.) and its kin are slender, long-tailed lizards found at elevations up to 8,500 ft. Often heard rustling among fallen leaves. Feed on grubs and insects.

DESERT SPINY SWIFTS (10 in. long) have a rough-and-ready appearance. They usually frequent rocky or brushy country, often climbing small trees. Eat insects, especially ants.

CHUCKWALLAS are large (16 in.), plant-eating lizards, whose edible flesh was prized by Indians. Change color somewhat with light and temperature. Use thick tail as club in defense.

WESTERN GROUND GECKO or **BANDED GECKO** (5 in. long), with fine scales and thin, transparent skin, squeaks when caught. Hides by day, hunts spiders and insects at night. Lays several small white eggs at one time.

WHIPTAIL LIZARDS (9 in.) or **RACERUNNERS,** with mottled, spotted markings, are found on open hillsides and sandy washes. Slender, short-legged. Common in deserts, under shrubs or loose rocks.

SNAKES OF MOUNTAIN AND MESA

BLUE RACERS (4 ft.), related to eastern Blacksnakes, often crawl with head raised. They are variable in color, slender and agile, often climbing bushes and trees after insects, lizards, and eggs.

GOPHER SNAKES (5 ft.) resemble common Bull Snakes of the prairies in appearance and habits, but occur up to 7,000 ft. in the Southwest. Feed on rodents.

CALIFORNIA KING SNAKE (4 ft.), glossy black, has bands of creamy white in chain-like pattern. Found in California and Southwest; makes docile pet.

WESTERN GARTER SNAKES (3 ft.) (three main groups) vary in color and markings. Common in moist places; emit foul odor when caught. Eat fish, toads, worms.

HOG-NOSED SNAKE (3 ft.), with upturned, shovel-like snout, burrows for food. Prefers toads. Hisses and puffs up in defense, or plays dead. Suitable as pet; it practically never bites.

HARMLESS SNAKES OF THE DESERT

RED RACER (4 ft.), slender and strong relative of Blue Racer, hunts in trees and shrubs. Color varies from red-brown to dark gray. Abroad in daytime, it eats insects, mice, lizards, and birds.

LONG-NOSED SNAKES (2½ ft.) eat small mammals and snakes. Hunt at night; often killed by cars. Long snout indicates burrowing; otherwise little is known of habits.

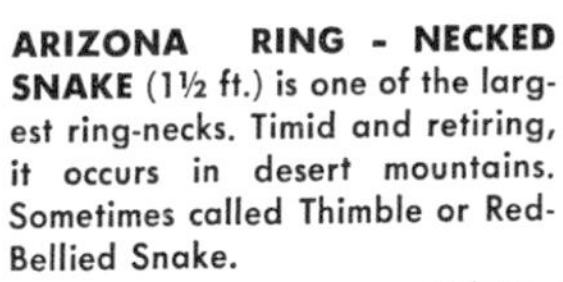

ARIZONA RING-NECKED SNAKE (1½ ft.) is one of the largest ring-necks. Timid and retiring, it occurs in desert mountains. Sometimes called Thimble or Red-Bellied Snake.

FANGLESS or **SPOTTED NIGHT SNAKE** (16 in.) lives—like related Fanged Night Snake—in rocky locations. Slightly poisonous saliva helps subdue small mammals.

MOUNTAIN KING SNAKE (3 ft.) inhabits Ponderosa Pine belt. Kills small mammals and snakes by squeezing. May kill and eat small rattlers, also birds and eggs. Resembles the more brilliant Coral Snake.

POISONOUS SNAKES

WESTERN DIAMOND-BACK RATTLESNAKES (5 ft.), aggressive and dangerous, are widely distributed on mesa and desert. Rattle loudly when disturbed. Contrasting pattern on tail. Eats small mammals. Young born alive.

PRAIRIE RATTLESNAKES (3½ ft.), of at least six intermixing races, are common in dry grasslands, often in prairie-dog towns. Gather in "dens" to hibernate.

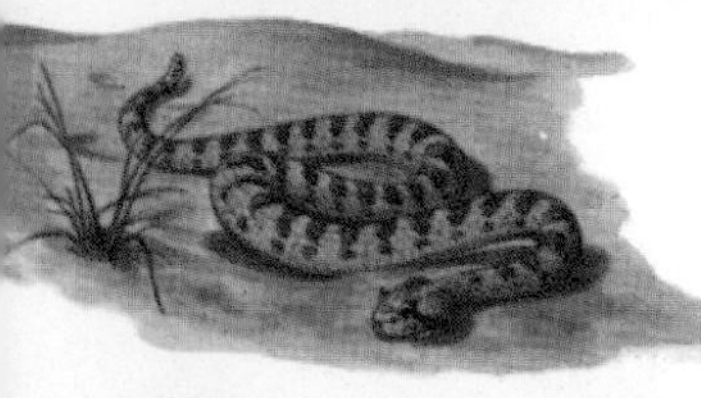

SIDEWINDER (2 ft.) travels in loose sand by winding or looping motion from side to side as it hunts small rodents at night. Rarely seen during day. Also called Horned Rattler for the hornlike ridge over each eye.

SONORAN CORAL SNAKES (18 in.), small, secretive, timid, are related to cobras. Poison is potent; could be deadly. No one bitten in Southwest so far as known. Identified by small head with black snout.

FIRST AID FOR SNAKE BITE Most visitors to the Southwest never see a rattlesnake. U-shaped pattern of tooth marks indicates non-poisonous bites; treat with a germicide. Double puncture of large fangs may confirm bite by poisonous snake. *Keep patient quiet;* send for doctor. Place tourniquet between bite and heart. Make ¼-in. X-cuts with sterile razor blade through each fang puncture. Maintain suction to promote bleeding. Loosen tourniquet briefly at 20-minute intervals.

GILA MONSTER (22 in.) is the only poisonous lizard in the U.S. Venom is secreted in lower jaw beneath the teeth. Although usually not dangerous, Gila Monsters can twist their heads and bite quickly. They should never be handled. Living in hot, dry desert flats or canyons, they remain in shade by day under brush or loose rocks. Feed on eggs, mice, lizards, young birds, rabbits.

TARANTULAS (body 1-2 in.) are feared because of size and appearance. Rarely bite humans; bite painful but not serious. Jump-and-attack stories are untrue. Live in small burrows.

DESERT CENTIPEDE (7 in.), a large species, has a poisonous but not dangerous bite. Treat bite with antiseptic to prevent infection. Widely distributed in Southwest.

BLACK WIDOW SPIDERS (1 in. over-all) are poisonous and sometimes deadly. Only females bite. Call doctor if bitten. Spiders make webs in dark corners, feed on insects.

SCORPIONS (1-5 in.) may be deadly to small children, painful to adults. Shake bedding and clothing when camping. If stung, apply ice and call doctor.

CARPENTER BEES (½-¾ in.), resembling blue-black bumblebees, burrow into dry wood — timbers, posts, telephone poles.

GREEN FRUIT BEETLES have large size (¾-1¼ in.) and bright metallic colors. They eat figs, apricots, grapes, other fruit.

TARANTULA HAWK (¾-1½ in.) is a black-and-red or brown metallic wasp. Harmless to humans, it preys on spiders to feed its young.

YUCCA MOTH (½-¾ in.), by pollinating yucca flowers, assures food for its young and seeds for the yucca. It flies at night.

WALKINGSTICKS (2-3½ in.), usually wingless, are slow, twiglike. Feed on broad-leaved trees; emit an odor offensive to birds.

Insects are everywhere and are especially numerous in frost-free desert climates. More kinds of insects are known than of all other animals. Some are helpful to mankind; others are injurious. Space permits only a brief introduction to a few of the thousands of species found in the Southwest.

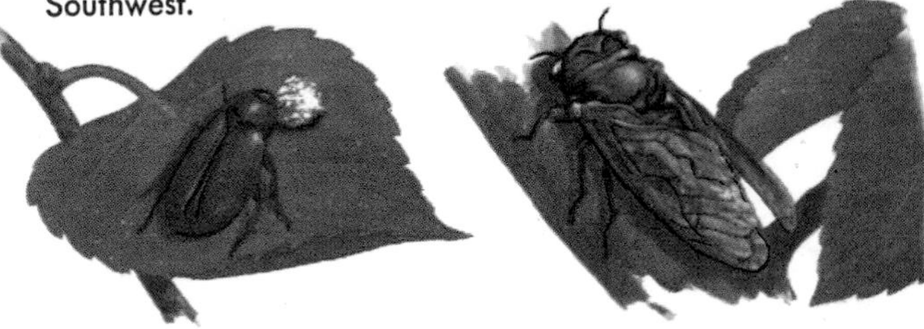

MAY BEETLES (1 in.) are robust, brown insects whose buzzing flight around lights attracts attention in early summer.

CICADA (1 in.) arouses curiosity with its shrill, vibrating song on hot summer days. Many species in Southwest.

BOXELDER BUG, common around Boxelder trees, is small (½ in.), flat. Young are bright red. Bug invades houses.

WHITE-LINED SPHINX MOTHS (2¼-4 in. wingspread), also called Hummingbird Moths, visit flowers at dusk, fearless of humans.

For more about insects read:

INSECTS, Essig, The Macmillan Co., N. Y., 1952.
INSECTS, Zim and Cottam, Golden Press, N. Y., 1956.
INSECT GUIDE, Swain, Doubleday, N. Y., 1948.

FIRE ANTS (1/5 in.) and some others sting savagely. Apply hot compresses and ammonia. Destroy the nests with a soil fumigant.

BUMBLEBEES (1 in.) rarely sting. Treat the painful puncture as above. The biggest of the bees, these make large nests under the ground.

YELLOW JACKETS (4/5 in.) usually nest underground. They can sting viciously. Treat wounds like ant stings; destroy nests with care.

HONEYBEES (1/2 in.) are beneficial pollen carriers. Many wild colonies exist in Southwest. Sting painful; in numbers they are serious; call a doctor.

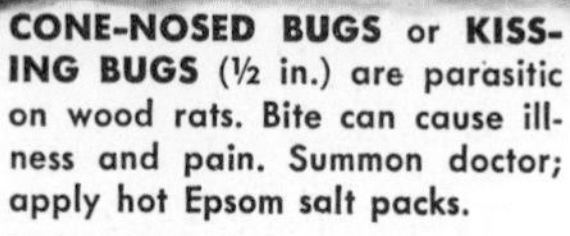

CONE-NOSED BUGS or **KISSING BUGS** (1/2 in.) are parasitic on wood rats. Bite can cause illness and pain. Summon doctor; apply hot Epsom salt packs.

Beaver: Largest of Rodents (34-35 in.)

WILD MAMMALS

Wild mammals of many kinds may be seen by watchful travelers. Beavers are increasing; elk are making a comeback; black bears occur in the mountains. In national parks and monuments, all mammals are protected in natural surroundings for you to observe and photograph. State and federal wildlife refuges (see p. 149) assure protection for a reservoir of game species. Diseases, parasites, food supply, animal and human enemies, and other natural factors produce population cycles among animals. All mammals, and plants or animals on which they feed, are involved in that complex interaction of all life and its environment which we call the Balance of Nature.

For more about Southwestern mammals read:

A FIELD GUIDE TO THE MAMMALS, Burt and Grossenheider, Houghton Mifflin Co., Boston, 1952.

LIVES OF GAME ANIMALS, Ernest Thompson Seton, Charles T. Branford Co., Boston, 1953 (6 vols.).

MAMMALS, Zim and Hoffmeister, Golden Press, New York, 1955.

ANIMALS OF THE SOUTHWEST DESERTS, Olin, Southwestern Monuments Assoc., Globe, Ariz., 1954.

MAMMALS OF NORTH AMERICA, Cahalane, The Macmillan Co., N. Y., 1947.

American Black Bear: Black, Brown, or Intermediate (200-400 lb.)

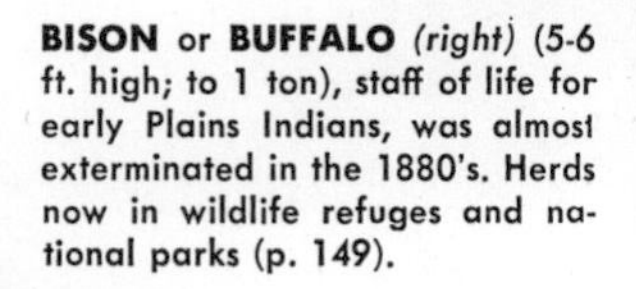

BISON or **BUFFALO** *(right)* (5-6 ft. high; to 1 ton), staff of life for early Plains Indians, was almost exterminated in the 1880's. Herds now in wildlife refuges and national parks (p. 149).

MULE DEER *(left)* (3-4 ft. high; 175-200 lb.), both desert and mountain species, are numerous; provide good hunting (p. 154). White-tailed Deer also are found in many desert mountain ranges.

PRONGHORNS or **ANTELOPE** *(right)* seem to be increasing. Bands may be seen in W Texas, E New Mexico, and central Arizona. Dwellers of open grasslands, they are alert and fleet.

BIGHORN or **MOUNTAIN SHEEP** *(left)* survive in rugged mountain refuges, favored by isolation and adequate grass and browse. Poachers, parasites, and wild burros are their enemies.

LARGE WILD MAMMALS

MOUNTAIN LIONS or **COUGARS** *(left)* (80-200 lb.; 6-8 ft. long) are large, powerful cats that prey on deer and livestock. Wide-ranging but timid, they persist in rocky and scrubby country despite trapping and hunting.

GRAY FOXES *(right)* (7-13 lb.) are predators which help control rodents. They are sometimes seen at night in national parks, where they have become accustomed to people. Smaller than Coyotes.

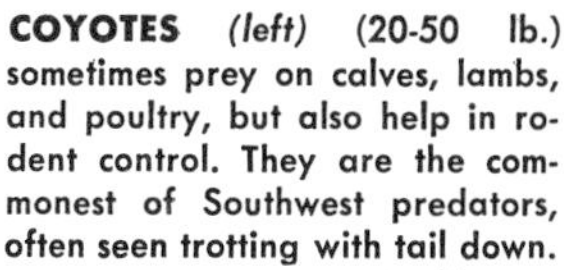

COYOTES *(left)* (20-50 lb.) sometimes prey on calves, lambs, and poultry, but also help in rodent control. They are the commonest of Southwest predators, often seen trotting with tail down.

BOBCATS *(right)* (15-25 lb.; 30-36 in. long), alert and stealthy, are abroad in rocky, brushy country day and night. They eat small mammals, birds — occasionally calves, lambs, poultry.

SMALL MAMMALS OF THE MOUNTAINS

YELLOW-HAIRED PORCUPINE *(right)* (25-30 in.), is common, clumsy; has quills on back and tail. Feeds mainly on herbs and inner bark of trees. Several races.

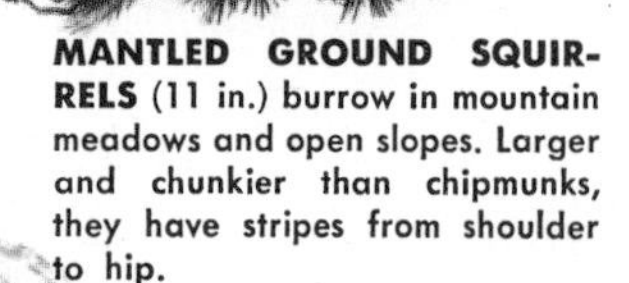

MANTLED GROUND SQUIRRELS (11 in.) burrow in mountain meadows and open slopes. Larger and chunkier than chipmunks, they have stripes from shoulder to hip.

CHIPMUNKS *(right)* (8 in.), vivacious, active rodents of several species, scamper over wooded and brushy slopes in search of fruits and insects. Five stripes from snout to tail.

MARMOTS or **ROCKCHUCKS** *(left)* (25 in.) live in colonies in mountain meadows and hillsides. Their call is a shrill whistle. Active all summer, they hibernate in winter.

SMALL MAMMALS OF THE MESAS

POCKET GOPHERS *(left)* (9 in.) are rarely seen. Their burrows, dug in search of roots, honeycomb grasslands and meadows. Destructive; hard to control.

TUFTED-EARED SQUIRRELS *(right)* are large (18 in.), handsome, gray inhabitants of Ponderosa Pine forests. Most famous is the Kaibab Squirrel of North Rim, Grand Canyon.

PRAIRIE DOGS *(left)* (15 in.) are chubby, short-tailed rodents of grasslands. Once common, they have been reduced by farming and poisoning. National and state parks provide sanctuaries.

BLACK - TAILED JACKRABBIT *(right)* (20 in.) really a long-eared hare, is prolific, wary, fleet, and able to obtain moisture from food. Population fluctuates in cycles. Destructive to crops.

SMALL MAMMALS OF THE DESERTS

KANGAROO RATS *(right)* (12 in.), abroad at night, have large heads, long hind legs and tails. Note their burrow mounds. They get all the water they need from plant food.

COATIS *(left)* (4 ft.), of the raccoon family, have long, upturned snouts useful in rooting for food. Their long tails are carried erect. Often travel in bands of 30 or more.

KIT FOXES *(right)*, small (30 in.), with large ears, are widespread but rarely seen. Night hunters, they investigate camps or search for mice and lizards among rocks and brush.

RINGTAILS *(left)* (28 in.) inhabit caves and ledges, hunting at night for rodents. Catlike in appearance, they are related to raccoons. Eyes and ears are large: tails, long and banded.

PLANT LIFE

Next to majestic scenery, it is the rich and varied plant life that captures your interest in the Southwest. Here grow giant Ponderosa Pines and weird, dwarf cactuses. Lush alpine meadows overlook barren, alkaline flats. You cannot but marvel at the unusual adaptations of Southwest plants to their varied environments. Their beauty is apparent, and in many places the plant cover soothes a harsh landscape.

The following pages emphasize typical plants of the Southwest, using elevation, as represented by the mountains, mesas, and deserts, as a key to grouping the flowering plants, shrubs, and trees. The cactuses and the plants confused with them are treated separately.

Time your Southwest visit to see most plants in bloom. Spring is blossom time on the desert. Flowers of mesas and mountains are showiest after summer rains. Enjoy flowers, photograph them, but let them grow and mature their seeds. Wildflowers and other plants are protected in all national and state parks.

For more about flowers read:

FLOWERS OF THE SOUTHWEST DESERTS, Dodge and Janish, 1952.
FLOWERS OF THE SOUTHWEST MESAS, Patraw and Janish, 1953.
FLOWERS OF THE SOUTHWEST MOUNTAINS, Arnberger and Janish, 1952.
(All above titles published by S. W. Monuments Assoc., Globe, Ariz.).
MEET THE NATIVES, Pesman, Smith Brooks Co., Denver, 1947.
FLOWERS, Zim and Martin, Golden Press, N. Y., 1950.
A TRAVELER'S GUIDE TO ROADSIDE WILD FLOWERS, Taylor; Farrar, Straus, and Young, N. Y., 1949.

COLORADO COLUMBINE (2-3 ft.) is one of many showy species in the Southwest. Blue-and-white Columbine, state flower of Colorado, blooms among aspens June to July.

HAREBELL (1-1½ ft.) is a delicate, nodding blue bellflower growing widely in clusters on open mountain slopes and moist meadows. Blooms from June to September.

WESTERN YARROW (12-20 in.) is a common mountain flower with finely divided leaves. Blooms from June to September on roadsides and grassy meadows. Indians use it medicinally.

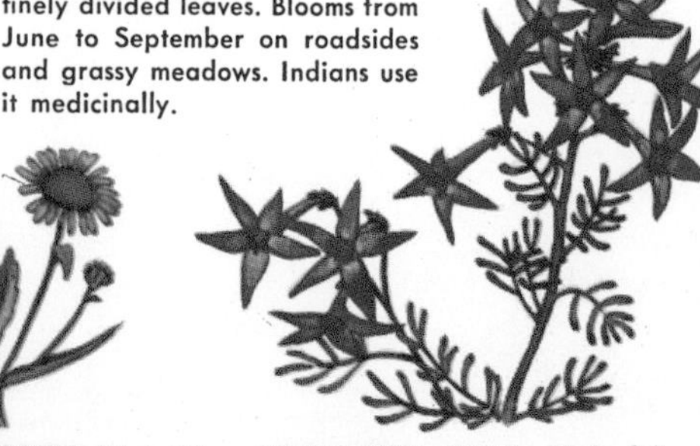

LEAFY-BRACT ASTER (½-4 ft.), yellow-centered, with blue or purple petals, is common along roads, slopes, and in forest meadows, August-September.

SKYROCKET GILIA (½-2 ft.), one of several common species with red, orange, or blue flowers, blooms throughout the summer in the Ponderosa Pine belt.

RICHARDSON GERANIUM (6-18 in.) blooms April-October in moist forest soil. Also called Cranesbill because of long beak on seed capsule. Relative of eastern woodland species.

SHOOTINGSTAR (6-18 in.) is a handsome flower of the primrose family growing singly or in clumps on stream banks or in moist places. Blossoms June through August.

SPREADING FLEABANE (4-20 in.) is often mistaken for an aster but has many more petals or rays. Common and widespread on lower slopes in summer and autumn.

COLUMBIA MONKSHOOD (3-5 ft.), tall, showy with deep blue, helmet-shaped flowers, contains poisonous alkaloids. Prefers open, moist places. Blooms June-Sept.

GENTIANS (6-18 in.), Blue and Fringed, are the queens of moist, open meadows in late summer and early fall. Roots have some medicinal value.

EVENING PRIMROSES (4 in.-4 ft.), both white- and yellow-flowered species, are common in summer and early fall. Blooms are large, loose, four-petaled.

LOCOWEED, or **MILKVETCH,** is one of many similar species (1-3 ft.). Pea-pod like flowers, white or cream to purple. Blossoms May-June. Some poisonous to livestock.

GAILLARDIAS (1-2 ft.) bloom May-October along roadsides and on sunlit flats among pines. Showy flowers, called "firewheels." Two common species.

CALABAZILLA GOURDS, like striped balls, develop from yellow, squash-like flowers. Vine, wide-spreading (10-15 ft.), has large, foul-smelling leaves.

WILD ZINNIA (½-1 ft.) makes golden patches on open flats, June-October. Hardy resident of dry mesas. Garden Zinnias come from Mexican species.

BLAZING-STAR (2-5 ft.) has 10-petaled flowers on slender, branching stems, open afternoons May-August. Clinging leaves give the name "Stickleaf."

SNAKEWEED (1-1½ ft.) covers rocky mesa tops with yellow clumps in late summer and fall. Unpalatable to livestock, its presence means overgrazed range.

GOLDEN CROWNBEARD (2-5 ft.) is the common yellow-centered, notch-petaled sunflower that fills field and roadside. Blooms late spring to November.

PALMER PENSTEMON (1-3 ft.), one of many western species, has flowers ranging from violet to scarlet. Common March-August, often on rocky hillsides.

ROCKY MOUNTAIN BEEPLANT (3-5 ft.) thrives along roadsides and fencerows, June-September. Crushed leaves smell bad; hence one other name—Skunkweed.

ARIZONA LUPINE, handsome blue finger-leaved pea, helps produce the desert's gorgeous spring display. Bluebonnet, state flower of Texas, also is lupine (1-3 ft.)

GOLDPOPPY or **CALIFORNIA POPPY** (4-18 in.), state flower of California, covers the spring desert with a cloth of gold after rainy winters. Mixes with lupine, Owl-clover, and other spring annuals.

DESERT - MARIGOLD, with its showy, long-stemmed, yellow, wheel-shaped flowers, makes bright golden patches at roadsides and in desert washes from March to October (1-2 ft.).

SACRED DATURA (1-3 ft.) has gray-green leaves and large, white, trumpet-shaped flowers, which close in sunlight. Indians used the narcotic seeds and roots.

PRICKLYPOPPY (2-3 ft.), with its tissue-paper-like petals, is unpalatable to livestock and indicates overgrazed range. Sap is yellow and sticky.

WILD-POTATOES (10-18 in.), some spiny, some smooth, with globular fruits, are widespread in summer. Other nightshades are common on mesas and prairies.

SANDVERBENAS (3-8 in.) carpet roadsides and sandy flats in spring. Fragrant pink to purple flowers grow in masses or mingle in the desert's gay color pattern.

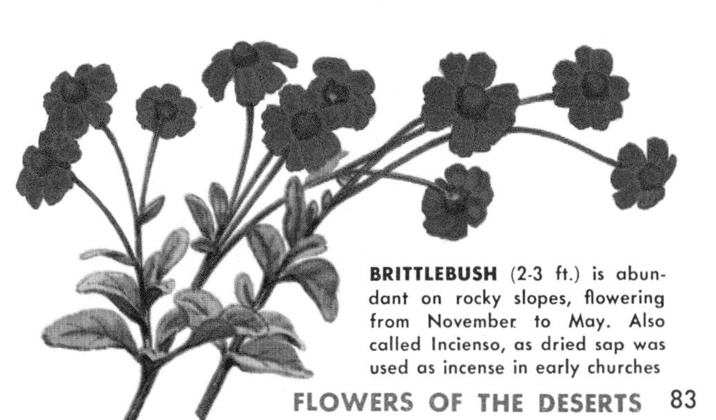

BRITTLEBUSH (2-3 ft.) is abundant on rocky slopes, flowering from November to May. Also called Incienso, as dried sap was used as incense in early churches

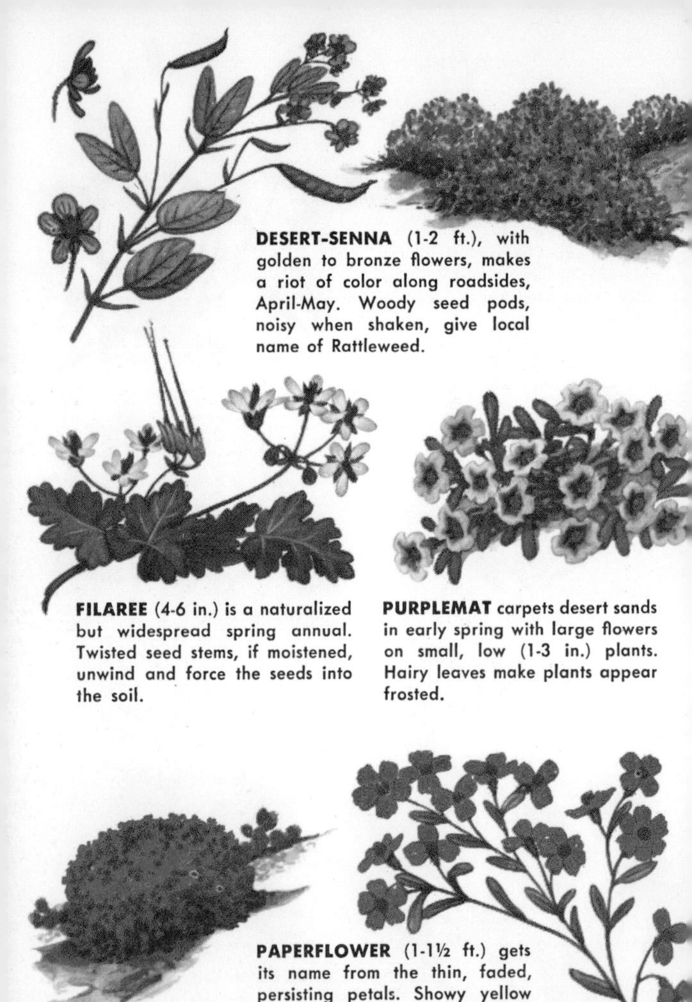

DESERT-SENNA (1-2 ft.), with golden to bronze flowers, makes a riot of color along roadsides, April-May. Woody seed pods, noisy when shaken, give local name of Rattleweed.

FILAREE (4-6 in.) is a naturalized but widespread spring annual. Twisted seed stems, if moistened, unwind and force the seeds into the soil.

PURPLEMAT carpets desert sands in early spring with large flowers on small, low (1-3 in.) plants. Hairy leaves make plants appear frosted.

PAPERFLOWER (1-1½ ft.) gets its name from the thin, faded, persisting petals. Showy yellow blossoms cover the plants, often in dry seasons when other flowers are absent.

CACTUSES

Cactuses (or Cacti) are Western Hemisphere succulents abundant in the Southwest. From tiny Button Cactus to 10-ton Saguaro (suh-WAR-oh), they are recognized by fleshy, leafless, green stems, often covered with clustered spines. Two hundred of the more than 1,200 species of cactus are native to the United States. Closest relatives are violets, oleasters, and passion flowers. Most cactus flowers are large, colorful, and attractive. Indians and desert animals eat the fruits. Stem cells store water after rains, and the plants' organs are designed to prevent loss of moisture. Some plants withstand 2 years of drought. Many Southwestern plants with spines, thorns, or sharp-pointed leaves are mistaken for cactuses. Four of them are pictured on p. 90.

For more information on cactuses read:

THE CACTI OF ARIZONA, Benson, Univ. of Arizona Press, Tucson, 1950.
THE CACTUS AND ITS HOME, Shreve, Williams & Wilkins Co., Baltimore, 1931.
THE FLOWERING CACTUS, Carlson, McGraw-Hill, N. Y., 1954.

SAGUARO or **GIANT CACTUS** (20-40 ft.), limited to S Arizona, is one of the Southwest's "trademarks." Arizona's state flower, it blooms in May. Fruit edible.

ORGAN PIPE CACTUS is found only in Southwest. Long (10-15 ft.) stems have many smaller ridges. Blossoms open at night in May.

SENITA CACTUS (4-8 ft.), a Mexican species, has shorter, less-fluted stems than Organ Pipe. In U.S., found only in Organ Pipe Cactus National Monument. Also called Whisker Cactus.

NIGHT-BLOOMING CEREUS (2-8 ft.) is drab but produces magnificent, fragrant white flowers, each open for one night in June or July. Has an immense, beet-like root.

CHRISTMAS CHOLLA (2-3 ft.) has long, thin joints, and grows in clumps. It produces attractive, olive-sized red fruits, which ripen in December.

TREE CHOLLA (CHO-yuh) 3-12 ft.) has loose branching joints that cling to anyone brushing against them; hence the alternate name, Jumping Cactus.

CANE CHOLLAS (3-8 ft.), of several species, are widespread up to 7,000 ft. Red- or bronze-flowered species are spectacular, May-July. Persistent yellow fruits.

TEDDYBEAR CHOLLA, small (2-5 ft.), tree-like, prefers hillsides. Dense, silvery spines look woolly. Fallen joints root. Flowers pale yellowish-green.

BEAVERTAIL CACTUS *(right)* has magenta flowers April to June. Low-growing (1-1½ ft.), it lacks spines. Small depressions give the flat joints a pocked appearance.

ENGELMANN'S PEAR *(left)* (1½-5 ft.) is the common, robust, yellow-flowered Prickly Pear, widespread in the Southwest. Mahogany-colored fruits, called "tunas," are edible when ripe.

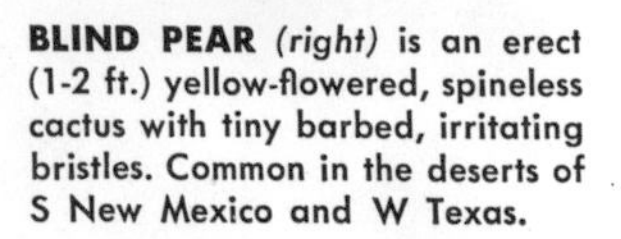

BLIND PEAR *(right)* is an erect (1-2 ft.) yellow-flowered, spineless cactus with tiny barbed, irritating bristles. Common in the deserts of S New Mexico and W Texas.

PURPLE TINGE PEAR *(left)* (1½-4 ft.), another high desert species, similar to Engelmann's, has purplish joints, especially during drouth or cold weather. Yellow flowers of one species have bright red centers.

BARREL CACTUSES *(left)* (1-6 ft.) are common in desert. Large ones like small Saguaros but with stout, hooked spines. Several species with pink, yellow, or orange flowers bloom May to September.

PINCUSHION CACTUSES *(right)* are similar to Fishhook species *(below)*, but they are globular and they grow singly or in clusters. They have short, flat-lying spines.

HEDGEHOG CACTUSES *(left)* form low (1-1½ ft.) clumps with the unbranched, cucumber-shaped stems. Flowers range from pink to magenta. Some blossom as early as March; most, later.

FISHHOOK CACTUSES *(right)* are small (2-10 in.). Several species produce tiaras of large, exquisite, lavender to purple flowers in early summer. Slender, curve-tipped spines resemble long-shanked fishhooks.

PLANTS CONFUSED WITH CACTUSES

CRUCIFIXION THORNS *(right)* are leafless, densely thorned desert shrubs (4-10 ft.) with green bark. Similar are Mohave Thorn and Allthorn.

YUCCAS (YUH-kuhs) *(left)*, narrow-leaf and broad-leaf, vary from small bushes to bulky trees; belong to the lily family. Stiff, sharp-tipped leaves and clusters of creamy flowers.

OCOTILLO (oh-ko-TEE-oh) *(right)* is a thorny shrub with long (8-12 ft.), whip-like, unbranched stems tipped in April-May with bright red flower clusters. Re-leafs after rain.

CENTURY PLANTS *(left)* form low crowns of stout, spine-tipped leaves. After years of food storage, plant produces 10-15 ft. flower stalk, then dies. Indians eat roasted bud stalk.

TREES AND SHRUBS

The Southwest possesses over 50 million acres of forested land. Pinyon and juniper woodlands cover many mesas; spruce, fir, and aspen clothe higher mountain slopes; and desert watercourses are lined with Mesquite thickets. The Colorado Plateau supports extensive commercial forests of Ponderosa Pine. Trees and shrubs grow at all elevations. The number, type, and size vary with temperature, moisture and topography.

Vegetative cover is vital in protecting watersheds, providing food and shelter for animals, and giving people hunting, fishing, and other recreational pleasures. Fire is a major forest enemy. Extinguish your campfires thoroughly, and put out all cigarettes and matches before discarding. Insects and tree diseases sometimes spread rapidly, destroying large areas of timber. Parasitic mistletoe is widespread, being very noticeable on junipers. It can kill or seriously damage valuable stands of commercial timber.

For more about Southwest trees and shrubs read:

ROCKY MOUNTAIN TREES, Preston, Iowa State Coll. Press, Ames, 1947.

SOUTHWESTERN TREES, U.S. Dept. Agr., Agricultural Handbook #9, Govt. Prtg. Office, Washington, D. C., 1950.

TREES AND SHRUBS OF SOUTHWEST DESERTS, Benson and Darrow, Univ. of N. Mex. Press, Albuquerque, 1954.

TREES, Zim and Martin, Golden Press, N. Y., 1956.

Juniper with Mistletoe

Mistletoe

MOUNTAIN CONIFERS

WHITE FIR *(right)* has a cone-shaped crown, short branches, and flat, silvery-green needles, which curve upward. Upright cones at top of tree. Common at 8,000-11,500 ft., it may grow 100 ft. tall.

SPRUCES *(left)* (80-100 ft.) form dense stands usually on north slopes, extending up to timber-line. Papery, pendent cones. Blue Spruce is state tree of Colorado.

DOUGLAS FIRS *(right)* are not true firs. Timber trees, up to 130 ft. tall, they are found in Southwest mountains up to 11,000 ft. Small ones are prized as Christmas trees.

PONDEROSA PINES *(left)* form open forests. Trees, valued for lumber, grow 4 ft. through, 180 ft. high. Needles 5-7 in. long, clusters of 2 or 3. Cones robust.

MOUNTAIN CONIFERS

LIMBER PINE *(left)* has a broad, open crown and long, plume-like branches. Trees, 25-50 ft. high, prefer ridges and open summits up to 12,000 ft. Needles 5 to a cluster. Hanging brown, thick-scaled cones, 4 to 8 in.

ALPINE FIR *(right)* is a tall (40-80 ft.), slender, spire-like tree found along alpine meadows. At timberline, dwarfed and twisted. Cones, upright, are deep purple.

FOXTAIL or BRISTLECONE PINE *(left)*, an alpine tree 30-40 ft. high, of irregular shape, often grows with spruces in thin, rocky soil. Needles short, 5 in a cluster.

LOW JUNIPER *(right)*, a spreading shrub, often grows under alpine trees. Foliage gray-green, scale-like. Often used in landscaping.

MOUNTAIN SHRUBS

POISON IVY *(right)* is found in moist canyons from 3,000 to 8,000 ft. Note the three shiny green leaflets. Look for it before making camp. Wash affected skin in strong soapy water.

BUCKBRUSH *(left)* forms low (3-ft.) thickets in pine forests. Deer browse foliage. Indians eat berries, make medicine from leaves. White flowers open April-October.

WESTERN THIMBLEBERRIES or **SALMONBERRIES** *(right)* are raspberry-like shrubs with large white blossoms. Found in pine forests or on spruce-dotted slopes. Birds eat the seedy fruits.

WATER BIRCH *(left)*, sometimes of tree size, often forms dense, shrubby thickets along streams. Lustrous bronze bark, rounded toothed leaves, and catkin-like flowers aid identification. The only native Southwest birch.

ARIZONA MOUNTAIN ASH *(left)*, an irregular shrub (6-10 ft.) of Transition and Canadian zones, rarely reaches tree size. Orange fruits are eaten by birds. Attractive; used in landscaping.

WILD RASPBERRIES *(right)*, ancestors of cultivated species, thrive in moist, rich soil of pine and spruce forests. Soft, red fruits enjoyed by man, beast, birds.

CHOKECHERRY *(left)* (15 to 25 ft.) may reach tree size and usually forms thickets along streams. This is a sacred plant of the Navajo Indians. Fruits are eaten by birds.

ALDER-LEAF MOUNTAIN MAHOGANY or **CERCOCARPUS** *(right)* (4 to 10 ft.) is recognized by fuzzy, twisted seed "tails." It prefers open, dry ridges in oak or white fir thickets. Sometimes browsed by deer.

ALDERS *(right)* sometimes grow to a height of 60 ft. and a trunk diameter of 3 ft., always in moist locations. Several species grow in mountains of the Southwest. Mountain alder (illustrated) is common.

QUAKING ASPENS *(left)*, mistaken for birch because of their white bark, take over mountainsides after forest fires. The leaves, on slender, flattened stalks, become a rich golden-yellow in autumn.

PEACHLEAF WILLOW *(right)*, found in moist locations, occasionally grows to a height of 30 ft. Other Southwest willows are also shrubs or small trees.

ROCKY MOUNTAIN MAPLE *(left)*, found as high as 9,000 ft. on moist hillsides, is small (rarely over 20 ft.). These maples are conspicuous in autumn as leaves turn scarlet.

UTAH JUNIPER *(left)*, in pure stands or with Pinyon Pine, marks upper Sonoran life zone. Rarely 20 ft. high. Used for fence posts or kindling. Commoner in Arizona and Nevada than New Mexico. Fruits purple to brownish.

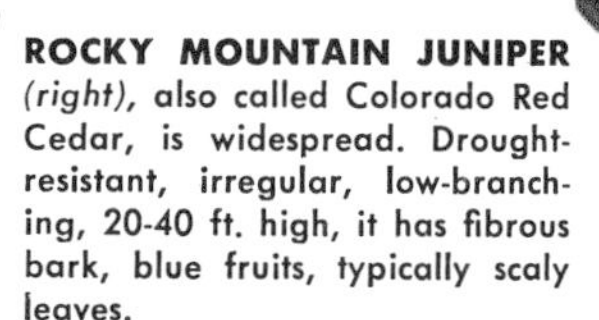

ROCKY MOUNTAIN JUNIPER *(right)*, also called Colorado Red Cedar, is widespread. Drought-resistant, irregular, low-branching, 20-40 ft. high, it has fibrous bark, blue fruits, typically scaly leaves.

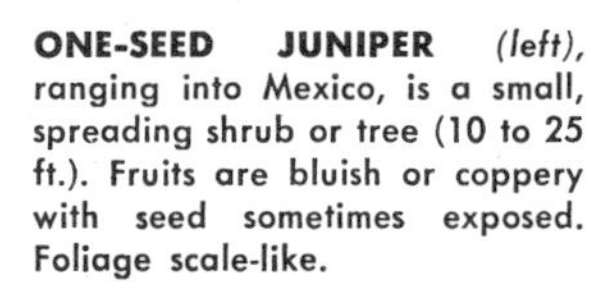

ONE-SEED JUNIPER *(left)*, ranging into Mexico, is a small, spreading shrub or tree (10 to 25 ft.). Fruits are bluish or coppery with seed sometimes exposed. Foliage scale-like.

ALLIGATOR JUNIPER *(right)* has furrowed, platy bark like alligator skin. Trees grow slowly. Large specimens, 30-50 ft. high, trunks up to 32 in., may be 500-800 years old. Red-brown fruit.

PINYON PINES The pungent odor of Pinyon (PIN-yon) smoke is a cherished memory to campers and old-timers. Pinyon wood was used for fuel by Pueblo Indians and by cliff dwellers before them. It was used by the Spanish and is still popular. Pinyon nuts, the seed of these pines, furnish food for wildlife, as well as for some Indians; Navajos travel many miles to harvest them after the cones open, September-October. Buy them at trading posts. The three species of Pinyon Pine are easily recognized by the number of needles in a bundle. The Singleleaf Pinyon grows in Nevada and Utah. The Colorado Pinyon (two needles) is widespread throughout the upper Sonoran zone. The Mexican Pinyon (three needles) ranges into western Texas and southeastern Arizona. Pinyons may grow in pure stands but often mingle with junipers and scrub oaks. They may reach a height of 30 to 50 ft. Trunks are short and twisting, and the crowns of older trees are spreading and branched. Wood is weak, brittle, and coarse-grained. Pinyon is the state tree of both Nevada and New Mexico.

INLAND BOXELDER *(left)*, sometimes 50 ft. tall, is a maple. Short-lived; subject to storm damage. Used as a shade tree, for it grows rapidly, even in poor soil. Thick, hairy, compound leaf, with three coarsely toothed leaflets.

NEW MEXICO LOCUSTS *(right)* (15-25 ft.) form thickets along foothill streams or with oaks on dry slopes. Sometimes planted as an aid in erosion control. Rose-colored, pea-like blossoms, in drooping clusters, open in May-June.

NARROWLEAF COTTONWOOD *(left)* and other cottonwoods (50-75 ft. high) border streams and washes on mesas and in canyons. Common throughout Southwest, these species are widely planted for shade.

GAMBEL-OAK *(right)* (15-35 ft.), with lobed leaves and scaly bark, is the common scrub oak of the mesas, growing alone or forming thickets with locusts and pinyons. Wildlife eat the acorns in winter.

SHRUBS OF THE MESA

UTAH SERVICEBERRY *(right)* (5-12 ft.) is widespread on mesas and foothills. Attractive white flowers open in April-May. Birds and Indians harvest the small juicy fruit; deer browse on leaves.

BIG SAGEBRUSH *(left)* (3-7 ft.), famous in song and story, occurs on Southwest mesas but is more common to the north. Note toothed leaves, shreddy bark, and tiny yellow flowers in fall.

RABBITBRUSH *(right)* (2-10 ft.; several species) may be mistaken for sagebrush except in September, when the coarse shrubs are covered with small, yellow, ill-smelling flowers.

APACHE PLUME *(left)* (3-6 ft.) affords browse for deer and livestock. White flowers in May, followed by plumed seed heads, aid identification. Helpful as a soil binder.

TESOTA or **DESERT IRON-WOOD** *(left)* (20-30 ft.), once common, has been decimated by use as firewood. Bears masses of lavender flowers in May. Edible seeds.

YELLOW PALOVERDE *(right)*, with golden spring blooms and green bark, is common along desert washes. Rarely 30 ft. tall, it is, like Mesquite, a member of the pea family.

CATCLAW ACACIA *(left)* (10-20 ft.) bears fuzzy yellow flowers April to October. It forms dense thickets on poor, dry canyon soils. Curved thorns give it the name Wait-a-Minute Bush.

MESQUITE (mess-KEET) *(right)* thickets line desert washes. Trees (15-25 ft.) have spiny twigs, delicate leaves, fragrant yellow flowers (April-May), and bean-like fruit pods.

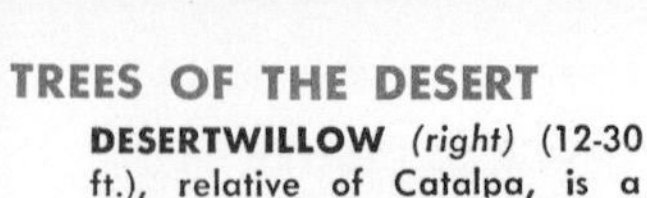

TREES OF THE DESERT

DESERTWILLOW *(right)* (12-30 ft.), relative of Catalpa, is a shrub or small tree covered in summer with orchid-colored flowers. Long, slender seed pods; very narrow, lance-shaped leaves.

TAMARISK *(left)* (several naturalized species) is spreading rapidly as a pest tree along watercourses. It endures alkaline soils and bears plume-like pink flower clusters in spring.

ARIZONA CYPRESS *(right)*, a beautiful evergreen (50-60 ft.), has drooping, graceful branches. It is found in canyon bottoms or on north slopes of desert mountains south into Mexico.

ARIZONA SYCAMORE *(left)* (60-80 ft.), with white, splotched trunks and spreading limbs, grows along streams in desert mountains. Soil-binding roots retard erosion. Blooms in April-May.

CREOSOTEBUSH *(left)* (4-11 ft.) is so widespread that it commonly marks the Lower Sonoran zone. Small yellow flowers, fuzzy white fruits, and glossy, paired, musty-smelling leaves. Twigs resinous; leaves "varnished" to reduce evaporation.

SALTBUSH *(right)* (2-4 ft.), often mistaken for sagebrush of higher elevations, grows in alkaline soils. Narrow, grayish leaves. Produces clusters of papery, 4-winged fruits.

MORMON-TEA *(left)* (2-4 ft.) grows on mesas as well as in deserts. Dried, the leafless stems made a tasty brew for early settlers. Inconspicuous yellow spring flowers attract insects.

WOLFBERRY *(right)* (3-6 ft.) is a stiff, thorny, winter-blooming shrub often becoming dormant in summer. Small, tomato-like fruits are eaten by birds and gathered by Indians.

SHRUBS OF THE DESERT

MESCALBEAN or **CORALBEAN** *(right)* (4-15 ft.), stout, has glossy green leaves and wisteria-like flowers. Woody seed pods hold 3-4 bright red, poisonous seeds.

JOJOBA (ho-HO-bah) *(left)* is a handsome, broad-leaved evergreen (3-6 ft.) abundant on dry slopes. An excellent browse plant, with acorn-like fruits which were eaten by Indians.

FAIRYDUSTER *(right)*, a sprawling, fine-leafed shrub (1-3 ft.), is common on dry slopes. Palatable to deer and valuable as a soil binder, it blooms from March to May.

SMOKETREE *(left)* (4-12 ft.) grows in sandy washes below 1,000 ft. Indigo flowers and slender, gray, drooping, leafless branches make it especially attractive in April and May.

San Francisco Peaks Near Flagstaff—Highest Point in Arizona

THE GEOLOGICAL STORY

The Southwest as a land began perhaps two billion years ago when the earth's crust formed. Rocks at the bottom of Grand Canyon are over a billion years old. For about 500 million years, much of the present Southwest was under shallow seas, and the deep sediments that piled up were slowly compressed into rock. The land rose and was submerged again and again. For the past 100 million years, most of the Southwest has been above water. Erosion wore down mountains, filling valleys with the debris, which was buried deep and hardened into rock. The great Rocky Mountain mass was pushed up, and huge volcanoes spewed lava and cinders over hundreds of square miles. While those building processes were at work, rain, wind, rivers, and ice were cutting away rock, wearing down valleys, gouging out canyons, and shaping the Southwest into the breath-taking scenery you see today. As part of this story, the geological history of the Southwest is outlined on pp. 106-107.

For more about rocks and earth history read:

PHYSIOGRAPHY OF WESTERN U.S., Fenneman, McGraw-Hill, N. Y., 1931.
DOWN TO EARTH, Croneis and Krumbein, Univ. of Chicago Press, 1936.
ROCKS AND MINERALS, Zim and Shaffer, Golden Press, N. Y., 1957.
THE ROCK BOOK, Fenton and Fenton, Doubleday & Co., N. Y., 1950.
ANCIENT LANDSCAPES OF THE GRAND CANYON REGION, McKee, 1952.

THE STORY OF THE EARTH

Geological Time Divisions	Millions of Years Ago	Characteristic Life of Period in Southwest	Major Events of This Time
Recent: Pleistocene	.015 to .025 1	Man came from Asia, using tools, language, and building a social system. Ground Sloth, Mammoth, Saber-Toothed Cat, and other mammals.	Activities of man, especially agricultural, changed the surface of the earth. Climate cold. Glaciers advance and recede.
Cenozoic: Pliocene Miocene Oligocene Eocene Paleocene	 13 25 36 58 63	Development of flowering plants. Mammals became important and spread over land and into sea. Early horses and camels.	Great period of mountain building. Rocky Mts. pushed up. Volcanoes in Rocky Mt. area. Much erosion. Climate became mild.
Mesozoic: Cretaceous Jurassic Triassic	 135 180 230	Backboned animals spread on land. Age of Reptiles marked by dinosaurs. First birds appeared. Land plants, such as cycads, palms, and simple conifers, developed.	Last great spread of the seas. Climate became cool. Period of erosion, with shallow seas covering small basins. Land often flooded and very swampy.
Paleozoic: Permian Pennsylvanian Mississippian Devonian Silurian Ordovician Cambrian	 280 310 345 405 425 500 600	Mosses and ferns became abundant on land, as plants and animals spread farther in seas. First backboned animals (fish) appeared. Amphibians and reptiles developed.	Climate cold, with glaciation. Lands low; seas and swamps spread, with alternate flooding and erosion. Thick sediments deposited. No mountain building.
Proterozoic: Keweenawan Huronian Temiskaming	 800 1,050 1,200	First clear and direct evidence of simple life in the sea—algae, bacteria, and protozoans.	Great eruptions, huge lava flows, and intrusive activity. Mountains uplifted and worn away. Glaciation.
Archeozoic: Laurentian Keewatin	 2,000 to 3,000	Indirect evidence of sunshine, rain, wind, clouds, oceans, rivers, and earth movements. No certain evidence of life.	Earth's crust gradually formed; continents and oceans developed. Continuous volcanic action.

IN THE SOUTHWEST

Where These Geological Formations May Be Seen

Principally volcanoes and sand dunes. San Francisco Volcanic Field. Near Grants, Carrizozo, and Raton, N. Mex. White Sands, Great Sand Dunes, Big Bend, Bandelier, Tonto, Petrified Forest, Lake Mead, and Death Valley.

Great Sand Dunes, Petrified Forest, Chiricahua, Organ Pipe Cactus, Tonto, Black Canyon of the Gunnison, Bandelier, Lake Mead, Death Valley, Big Bend, Bryce Canyon, Cedar Breaks, and many other places.

Mesa Verde, Big Bend, Tonto, Capulin Mt., Chiricahua, Death Valley, Rainbow Bridge, Arches, Black Canyon of the Gunnison, Navajo, Capitol Reef, Cedar Breaks, Petrified Forest, Grand Canyon, Zion, Canyon de Chelly, Colorado Nat. Mon., and many other locations.

Carlsbad Caverns, Big Bend, Grand Canyon, Lake Mead, Canyon de Chelly, Walnut Canyon, Natural Bridges, Organ Pipe Cactus, Death Valley, and many other locations.

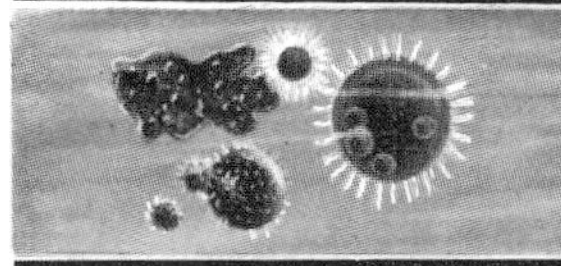

Death Valley, Great Sand Dunes, Organ Pipe Cactus, Tonto, Lake Mead, Grand Canyon, Black Canyon of the Gunnison, Chiricahua, Colorado Nat. Mon., and other locations.

Great Sand Dunes, Chiricahua, Black Canyon of the Gunnison, Lake Mead, Grand Canyon, and some other places.

ANCIENT LIFE IN THE SOUTHWEST has been traced back for over 500 million years. The first simple life was in the sea. More spectacular have been the backboned animals living here during the last 200 million years. These have included fish, amphibians, reptiles, and mammals.

TITANOTHERES — large, extinct mammals related to early horses and rhinoceros. Many species in North America; this one from Death Valley Oligocene rocks.

ERYOPS, a heavy, 5-ft.-long amphibian, is found in Permian beds of Texas. A marsh dweller, with strong, sturdy legs well adapted for life on land.

MAMMOTH was one of the widespread hairy elephants of Pleistocene times. Definite evidence exists that early man hunted these ice-age beasts.

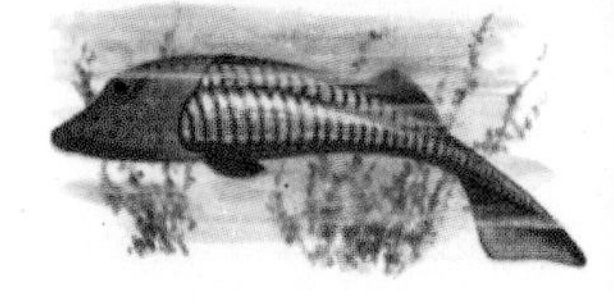

CEPHALASPIS, an armored Devonian fish, grew 1-2 ft. long (some kinds larger). Typical descendant of first backboned animals. Fossils from Colorado.

TYRANNOSAURUS, of the Cretaceous period, was 20 ft. high. Not the largest dinosaur, it was the most fearsome, with great claws and teeth.

Numerous dinosaur remains have been found in western North America, among them some of the largest known. Dinosaur tracks, remains of their skeletons, and fossils of other sea and land animals and early plants may be seen in local museums in the Southwest.

GROUND SLOTH was a huge, clumsy plant-eater of the Pleistocene. Bones, skin, dung, and hair have been found in caves, some near human remains.

GLYPTODONTS, contemporaries of the Ground Sloth, included this heavily armored and armed relative of the Armadillo, 8 to 10 ft. long. Once widespread.

PHYTOSAURS, reptiles of crocodilian appearance, were common in the Triassic. Not ancestors of living crocodiles. Probably fish-eaters.

EOHIPPUS (ee-oh-HIP-us), first of the horses, had toes instead of hoofs. About the size of a small dog. Common on Southwestern prairies in Eocene time.

MOSASAURS, marine lizards, 15-20 ft. long, roved shallow Cretaceous seas. Many species, mainly fish-eaters, occur in Texas chalk beds.

Specimens of Petrified Wood

PETRIFIED WOOD occurs widely. Spectacular deposits are found in the Southwest (see p. 127). Here, 160 to 180 million years ago, grew huge forests of Araucaria Pines. Many trees decayed where they fell, but some were carried away by streams to be stranded and later buried in sand, mud, or volcanic ash. Deposits 3,000 ft. thick accumulated over them when shallow seas covered the region. Through complicated natural processes the wood cells were infiltrated with silica-bearing water. Cell structure, annual rings, and other features of the original wood have thus been retained in the agate that formed. Silica is colorless, but traces of iron, manganese, and other minerals gave it shades of yellow, blue, red, and brown. The petrified logs lay buried for millions of years. Uplift of the region when the Rocky Mountains were formed accelerated erosion, and the petrified trunks were uncovered; many of them were cracked into uniform lengths by earth tremors. Some agatized wood takes a beautiful polish and is used in jewelry.

ROCK AND MINERAL WEALTH has colored the Southwest's past and helped make the region, including its marvelous scenery, what it is today. Rocks are natural materials forming the earth's crust. Minerals are chemical elements or inorganic compounds found in nature. Most rocks are composed of minerals. By studying rocks, scientists learn of conditions that prevailed at the time these materials were formed. Minerals are a source of valuable metals and nonmetallic chemical compounds.

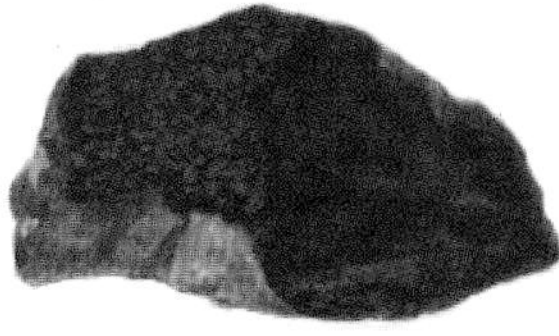

FOOL'S GOLD (iron pyrites) *(left)* is iron sulfide, common in veins. Hard and brittle, it fools amateurs but not miners. Occasionally fool's gold is associated with gold deposits.

CALCITE *(right)*, calcium carbonate, in many forms, accompanies other minerals in veins. It is found as clear or tinted crystals. Dissolves with bubbles in weak acid.

GYPSUM *(left)*, calcium sulfate, is often found in clay as single or fish-tailed crystals of selenite. Also common as soft, white layers in some sediments formed under arid conditions.

TURQUOISE *(right)*, found in veins in arid lands, is the gem stone of the Southwest. Long prized by Indians, it is now sold widely in jewelry. Beware of cheap stones and imitations.

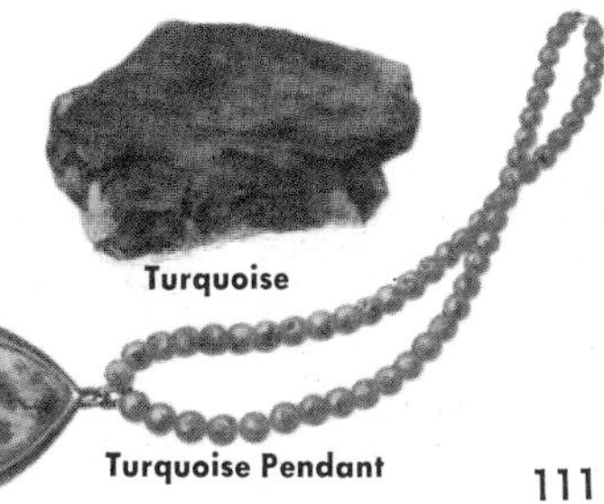

Turquoise

Turquoise Pendant

Turquoise Bracelet

Opal in Matrix

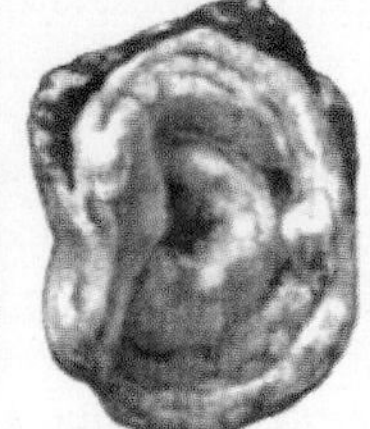
Chalcedony

Moss Agate

Jasper

QUARTZ, or silica, world's most common mineral, occurs in sand, sandstone, and other rocks. Milky Quartz fills veins, may indicate presence of gold. Crystals of quartz, always 6-sided, are found in rock cavities. Smoky Quartz is gray to black; Amethyst, purple. Jasper, agate, chalcedony (kal-SED-nee), and flint are noncrystalline. Opal contains water, never forms crystals; it may be colorless or have rainbow tints. Chalcedony is translucent, waxy, usually gray or dull; it lines cavities or forms concretions. Moss Agate is light-colored translucent or clouded agate with included dendrites, suggesting moss. Jasper is opaque chalcedony, yellow or brown with bands or irregular markings. Mason and Llano Counties, Tex., contain nearly 100 different gem materials, including quartz forms. Gem Village, 18 miles east of Durango, Colo., is the center of a rich rock-collecting territory.

For other Southwest gem localities see GEM HUNTERS' GUIDE, MacFalland Chagnon, Science and Mechanics Publishing Co., Chicago, 1953.

Rose Quartz

Crystal Quartz

Amethyst

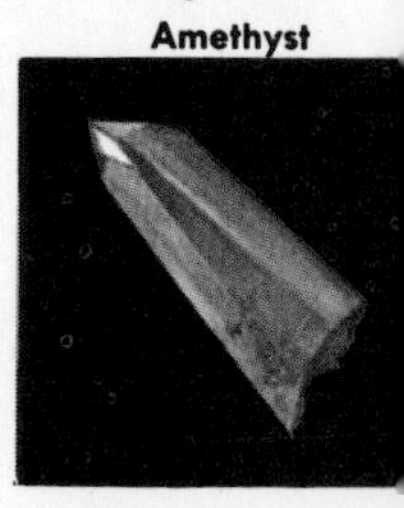

ORES of the Southwest have yielded many millions of dollars in precious and useful metals. Mining brought people to the Southwest, and it is still an important industry, though activity fluctuates with demand. Gold, copper, lead, silver, zinc, uranium, vanadium, and wolfram are the major metals. Nonmetallic products include feldspar fluorite, coal, pumice, gypsum, bentonite, asbestos, sulfur, mica, potassium, sand, and gravel. Petroleum and natural gas are also of first rank.

ZINC ORE, sphalerite, zinc sulfide, is yellow to dark brown, glassy, shiny. Occurs in veins, often with galena. This zinc ore slowly changes into other zinc minerals.

LEAD ORE, galena, is lead sulfide, a brittle, heavy, silvery mineral. In the Southwest, galena often contains silver. Other lead ores form from galena by action of air and water.

SILVER is sometimes found as the native element, more often as argentite, a silver-sulfur compound. In the Southwest, silver occurs with lead and zinc ores.

GOLD, not of great importance in the Southwest, is heavy, soft, and yellow. In most gold ore, the gold is minute. Chances of finding visible gold are remote.

Azurite and Malachite

COPPER, used since ancient times, is important in the Southwest, where the great open-pit mines are world-famous. Copper sometimes occurs as the soft native metal. Most important of the Southwest ores, malachite (green) and azurite (blue) are often found together and are occasionally of gem quality. Chrysocolla, a compound of copper and silica found with quartz and resembling turquoise, is sometimes used for jewelry. Chalcopyrite, an ore of copper, sulfur, and iron, is similar to iron pyrites (p. 111) but is yellower.

Chrysocolla Chalcopyrite

URANIUM ORE may contain up to about half its weight in uranium. The soft, crumbling, yellowish ore, carnotite, has long been known in the Southwest and is now mined in the "Four Corners" area. Few deposits are rich; the search for richer ones continues.

Carnotite

FLUORITE, or calcium fluoride, is used in the steel, aluminum, and chemical industries. It occurs as yellow, green, blue, and purple masses in sedimentary rocks and in ore veins. Cubic crystals are common. Too soft for gem use, fluorite is carved for lamps and ornaments.

Fluorite

SEDIMENTARY ROCKS are the commonest of the rocks that form the basic structure of the earth's surface. They are made of debris, or organic or chemical deposits. Some are coarse, but commoner in the Southwest is sandstone, made in ancient deserts, lakes, and seas of cemented grains of sand. Shale is a hardened mudstone. Limestone, widely deposited and usually fine-grained, was formed from remains of shellfish or through chemical action in shallow seas. In the dry Southwest it caps some mesas and plateaus.

Sandstone

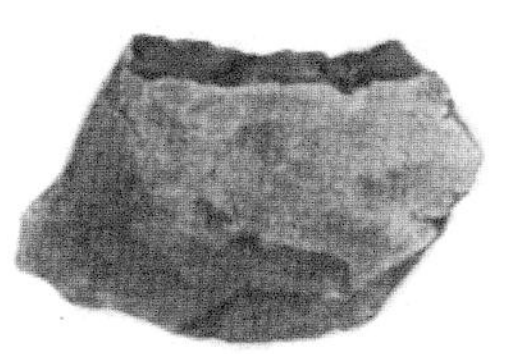

Limestone

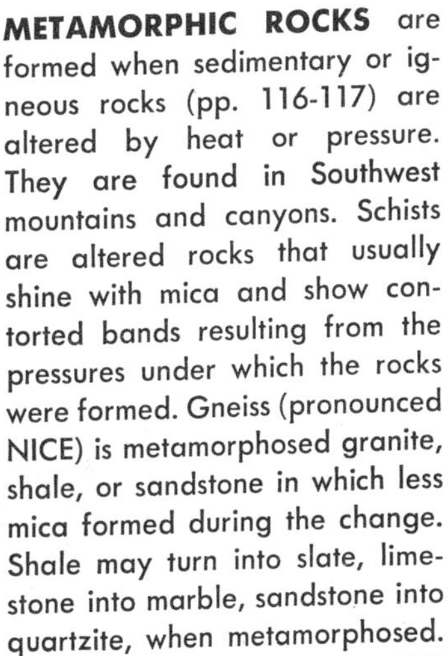

METAMORPHIC ROCKS are formed when sedimentary or igneous rocks (pp. 116-117) are altered by heat or pressure. They are found in Southwest mountains and canyons. Schists are altered rocks that usually shine with mica and show contorted bands resulting from the pressures under which the rocks were formed. Gneiss (pronounced NICE) is metamorphosed granite, shale, or sandstone in which less mica formed during the change. Shale may turn into slate, limestone into marble, sandstone into quartzite, when metamorphosed.

Gneiss

Schist

Granite

Diabase

Felsite

IGNEOUS ROCKS are more widespread in the West than elsewhere. They form from material in or beneath the earth's crust which becomes molten. This thick liquid (magma) varies chemically and produces different rock types. If it cools slowly within the earth's surface, it crystallizes into minerals, including ores. Granite, usually made of feldspar, quartz, and mica, is such a rock. Diabase, containing more of the dark minerals, is common in the formations known as dikes and sills. If lava pours out onto the earth's surface and cools fast, rocks formed are fine-grained. Most result from volcanoes and are hard to identify. Light, pink, gray, or yellow fine-grained ones are called felsite. Obsidian, glassy black or brownish, is lava that cooled fast. Gas bubbles in lava may make a froth that cools as pumice, so light that it floats. Common black lava, basalt, occurs widely in many forms.

Obsidian

Pumice

Basalt

Active Volcanoes Were Once Numerous in the Southwest

VOLCANOES AND LAVA FLOWS dot the Southwest. Only remnants remain of old volcanic fields, but recent volcanoes retain their original structure. Cinder cones are common, as are larger volcanoes made of mixed cinders and lava, such as those of the San Francisco Mountains near Flagstaff, Ariz. Recent lava flows look like frozen rivers of black basalt. Others, much older, form the hard caps that have protected great stretches of land from erosion and today form the dark-capped buttes, mesas, and tablelands. (See p. 131.)

Major Volcanic Fields

1 San Francisco
2 Datil—Mt. Taylor
3 Spanish Peaks—Capulin
4 Mt. Trumbull
5 Carrizozo
6 Jemez Mountain
7 Chiricahua Mountain
8 Death Valley
9 Pinacate
10 Davis Mountain
11 High Plateau
12 Hopi Buttes and Navajo

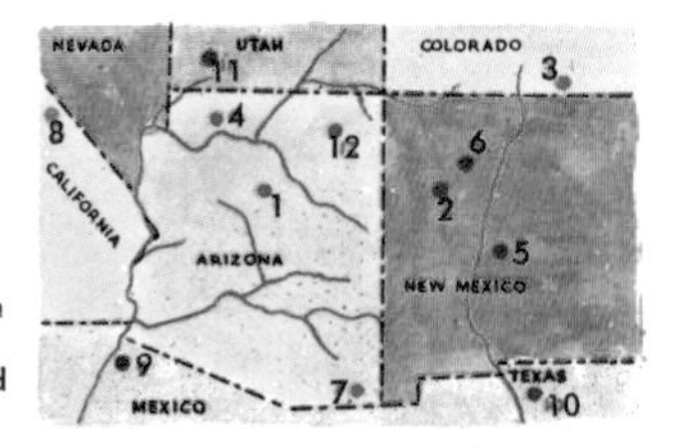

Mountains Formed by Erosion

Mountains Formed by Folding and Thrust-faulting

Mountains Formed by Block-faulting

MOUNTAIN MAKING involves complex processes well illustrated in the Southwest. Volcanic mountains are numerous (see p. 117). Where immense areas were evenly lifted, rivers carved wide valleys, leaving buttes and mesas. Squeezing and folding pressures forced older layers up, sometimes pushing them over younger ones. Terrific tensions produced jagged breaks in the earth's crust, and huge blocks were lifted and tilted. Chiseled by erosion, block-fault mountains form the rugged basin-and-range topography of western Utah and eastern Nevada. The Rocky Mountains represent up-bulging of a great rock complex. Erosion has stripped off the covering layers, whose tilted stumps are the hog-back foothills paralleling both sides of the hard core—the Rockies proper.

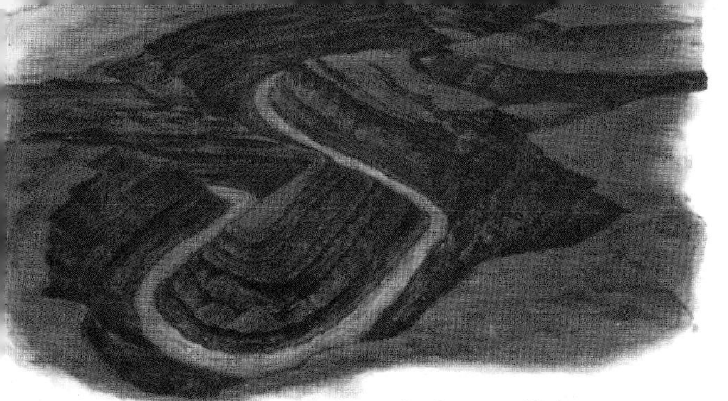

Gooseneck of San Juan River, Southeastern Utah

EROSION, THE GREAT LAND SCULPTOR Water, wind, frost, and gravity have carved and shaped the Southwest in a slow, never-ending process. Mountains have been reduced to plains, though lavas and hard sedimentary rocks protect the older uplands. Soft shales and clays have been carved intricately, as in Bryce Canyon, and have been flushed from beneath harder layers that have broken off to form cliffs. Water, fortified with gravel, is the principal agent wearing down and carrying away land. Where land has been consistently rising, the cutting power of streams is maintained in their original channels. Classic examples are the Grand Canyon of the Colorado and "goosenecks" of the San Juan. Such activities as clearing of land accelerate erosion in many areas.

Camel Rock, North of Santa Fe

WHAT TO SEE AND DO

Everywhere you look, there's something to see. The next pages spotlight important attractions, from citrus groves to trout streams, from cactus deserts to ski runs. For touring ideas see pp. 8-16. For a broader view of the region try the "American Guide Series":

TEXAS, Hastings House, N. Y., 1949.
OKLAHOMA, Univ. of Okla. Press, Norman, 1945.
KANSAS, Hastings House, N. Y., 1949.
COLORADO, Hastings House, N. Y., 1951.
NEW MEXICO, Univ. of N. Mex. Press, Albuquerque, 1945.
UTAH, Hastings House, N. Y., 1941.
NEVADA, Binfords and Mort, Portland, Ore., 1940.
ARIZONA, Hastings House, N. Y., 1949.
CALIFORNIA, Hastings House, N. Y., 1943.
Also:
THE SOUTHWEST, editors of LOOK, Houghton Mifflin, Boston, 1947.

Among periodicals the following are of particular interest:

DESERT MAGAZINE, Palm Desert, Calif.
ARIZONA HIGHWAYS, Ariz. State Highway Dept., Phoenix, Ariz.
NEW MEXICO MAGAZINE, State Capitol, Santa Fe, N. Mex.
NEVADA HIGHWAYS AND PARKS, Dept. of Highways, Carson City, Nev.
ARIZONA STATE PARKS, 1610 W. Adams, Phoenix, Ariz.

Before starting Southwestward, write to any of the following for road maps and specific information. If you are to travel by railroad, bus line, or airline, consult the one you plan to use. Major gasoline companies provide maps and will aid in your planning.

New Mexico Tourist Bureau, State Capitol, Santa Fe, N. Mex.
Colorado Department of Public Relations, State Capitol, Denver, Colo.
Associated Civic Clubs of Southern Utah, Richfield, Utah.
Arizona State Highway Department, Phoenix, Ariz.
Nevada Department of Highways, Carson City, Nev.
California Dept. of Natural Resources and Parks, Sacramento, Calif.
Texas State Parks Board, 106 E. 13th St., Austin, Tex.
Kansas Industrial Development Comm., 801 Harrison St., Topeka, Kan.
Okla. Plan. and Res. Bd., 533 State Capitol, Oklahoma City, Okla.
National Park Service, Southwest Region, Box 1728, Santa Fe, N. Mex.
U.S. Forest Service, Reg. Forester, Federal Bldg., Albuquerque, N. Mex.

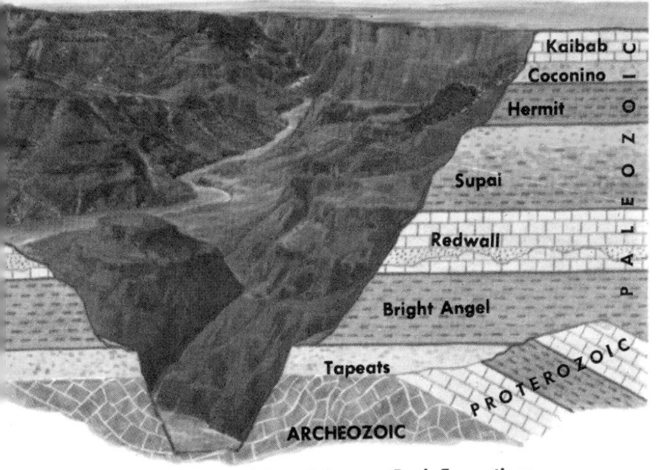

Cross Section of Grand Canyon Rock Formations

GRAND CANYON is a great gash in the earth 217 miles long, 4-18 miles wide, and 1 mile deep, cut by the Colorado River through the Kaibab Plateau of northwestern Arizona. View it from either rim or from the air. Its rugged interior is accessible by foot or horseback. The South Rim (elev. 6,900 ft.) may be reached the year round by bus, rail, or auto and in summer by air. A hotel, auto lodge, and campground provide accommodations. The North Rim (8,200 ft.) is closed by snow in winter. Cabins, cafeteria, and campgrounds are open May 15-Oct. 15. Cedar City, Utah, is the nearest approach by plane and train. To be sure, make reservations in advance. Saddle-horse trips and bus tours are available, and the National Park Service provides free lectures and museum services. Discovered by Coronado's followers in 1540 and explored by John Wesley Powell in 1869, Grand Canyon was made a national park in 1919. Wild animals abound. Typical plants of the mesas may be seen.

BRYCE CANYON NATIONAL PARK has spectacular amphitheaters eroded from the Pink Cliffs of the Paunsaugunt Plateau, southwest Utah. Paved roads and trails. Facilities: public campground, cabins, cafeteria, lodge; museum; Ranger guide service. Facilities closed in winter; roads are kept clear; park stays open. Nearest railhead and airport: Cedar City.

ZION NATIONAL PARK has a 2,000-3,000 ft. gorge in red and white Mesozoic rocks of the Kolob Plateau, southwest Utah. Massive cliffs and gorgeous panoramas mark the Virgin River. Mt. Carmel Highway connects U.S. 89 with U.S. 91. Accessible by auto or bus from Cedar City. Cabins, cafeteria, and campground in park and nearby Springdale open all year. Museum; field trips; campfire programs. Paved highways; 26 miles of trails.

For other spectacular canyon scenery, visit:
Salt River Canyon, on U.S. 60 north of Globe, Ariz.
Fish Creek Canyon, on the Apache Trail (Arizona State Highway 88).
Aravaipa Canyon (hikers only), Mammoth, Ariz.
Black River Canyon, near Ft. Apache, Ariz.
San Juan Goosenecks, Mexican Hat, Utah.
Rio Grande Canyon, south of Taos, N. Mex.

BLACK CANYON OF THE GUNNISON, in west-central Colorado, has breath-taking depths and a vast expanse of sheer walls of granite and schist. Accessible from Crawford (north) and Montrose (south); roads may be impassable in winter. Only accommodations are campgrounds.

THE ROYAL GORGE of the Arkansas River has long been a major attraction of southern Colorado. It is spanned by a long, extremely high suspension bridge reached from Canyon City on the east and Salida on the west, on U.S. 50. The hanging railroad bridge within its depths is notable.

CEDAR BREAKS' huge bowl is carved from the same colorful rocks as Bryce Canyon, 95 miles east. Lacking Bryce's delicate formations, it has, however, more color variety. Cedar Breaks Lodge is open June 15-Sept. 10. Roads are closed by snow Nov.-May. Cedar City is railhead and airport.

OAK CREEK CANYON, Ariz., is 10 spectacular miles (U.S. 89A) between Flagstaff and Sedona within a great lava-rimmed gash in the Coconino Plateau. Along tree-shaded banks of a brawling trout stream within its depths are small orchards and farms, restful guest ranches, and resorts.

Santa Elena Canyon

BIG BEND NATIONAL PARK, one of the newest and the only one in Texas, is separated from Mexico by only the narrow Rio Grande, which has cut five rugged canyons in its southward swing around the lofty Chisos Mountains. Big Bend combines sweeping views; interesting animals such as the Kit Fox and Peccary; Century Plants and others equally weird; the gentle winter climate of the Chihuahuan Desert; and the atmosphere of old Mexico. Its peaks (nearly 8,000 ft.) offer a cool retreat in summer. The park may be entered by paved highway from either Alpine or Marathon (118 and 80 miles away, respectively), both on the Southern Pacific Railway. A public campground, restaurant, and limited cabin accommodations are available the year round. Horse and foot trails lead to points of interest. Fish in the Rio Grande, or picnic on its northern bank. On Dagger Flat, in April, the huge Giant Dagger Yucca blossoms in profusion, except during periods of drouth. Park Rangers provide information for visitors and protection for park features.

COLORADO NATIONAL MONUMENT contains a colorful array of canyons, amphitheaters, cliffs, and pinnacles. It illustrates faulting, a great hiatus, and erosion. A paved loop highway from Grand Junction to Fruita in west-central Colorado makes it accessible along a spectacular rim drive. Campgrounds only.

CAPITOL REEF NATIONAL MONUMENT, a vast region in Wayne County, Utah, is named from a long, highly colored cliff face resulting from erosion of the famous Waterpocket Fold. State Highway 27, a graded dirt road, crosses the area. Trails lead into scenic canyons. Accommodations at Torrey and Fruita.

MONUMENT VALLEY, named for huge pinnacles and majestic erosional remnants, is in the Navajo Reservation on the road from Kayenta, Ariz., to Bluff, Utah. Be prepared to camp if necessary. Trading posts provide some facilities, including gasoline and guide service.

DEADHORSE POINT overlooks canyon grandeur rivaling that of Grand Canyon. Near the junction of the Colorado and the Green Rivers, it is reached by dirt road leaving U.S. 160 at a point 12 miles north of Moab, Utah. The road continues beyond the Point to other overlooks.

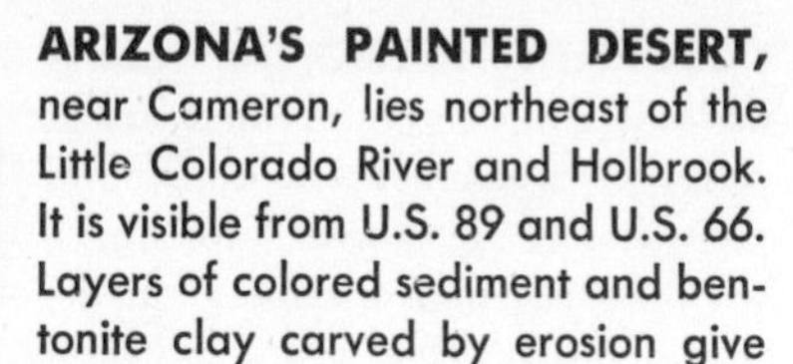

ARIZONA'S PAINTED DESERT, near Cameron, lies northeast of the Little Colorado River and Holbrook. It is visible from U.S. 89 and U.S. 66. Layers of colored sediment and bentonite clay carved by erosion give the colorful banded effect.

CHIRICAHUA (CHEERY-cow-ah) **NATIONAL MONUMENT** is the Wonderland of Rocks of southeastern Arizona. Erosion in columnar lavas of the Chiricahua Mountains has created a jumble of grotesque rock figures accessible by highway and 14 miles of trails. Horses and limited accommodations available.

VALLEY OF FIRE STATE PARK protects an amazing outcrop of huge brick-red rock fins reached by a short dirt road from Overton, Nev. Along the trails, this maze resembles a city of crooked streets winding between rows of tall, red-brick buildings. Picnic facilities.

VALLEY OF THE GOBLINS, a paradise for back-country explorers, is accessible only by jeep or pickup truck over a 38-mile dirt route starting at Hanksville, Utah. Take food and water. Another spectacular isolated area, Cathedral Valley, is reached via Fremont, Utah.

PETRIFIED FOREST NATIONAL MONUMENT, site of the largest and most colorful concentrations of petrified wood in the world, lies between U.S. 66 and U.S. 260, 20 miles east of Holbrook, Ariz. State Highway 63, traversing the monument, is closed at night to protect the petrified wood. Visitors are urged to resist temptation and leave the wood for others to enjoy. In addition to the quantities of agate, jasper, and chalcedony (see p. 112) found in the six forests, there are badlands of colored clays that have weathered into a haunting Painted Desert landscape (p. 126). A fine museum is located half a mile from the U.S. 260 entrance, with a small restaurant, a curio store, and limited overnight accommodations nearby. Trains stop at Holbrook, where automobiles may be hired. Nearest airports: Winslow, Ariz., and Gallup, N. Mex.

Other petrified forests in the Southwest:
Sweet Ranch, southwest of Santa Fe, N. Mex.
Near Tascosa, in the Texas Panhandle.

WHITE SANDS NATIONAL MONUMENT, in south-central New Mexico, 146,535 acres, is covered by drifts of gleaming white gypsum sand—home of a few struggling plants and a rare lizard and a pocket mouse, both white. It is accessible from U.S. 70. There is a picnic area; overnight accommodations are available in Alamogordo. An excellent loop road begins at the park museum, where a series of exhibits illustrates the geology and the natural history of this unique area.

GREAT SAND DUNES NATIONAL MONUMENT has 600-ft. drifts along the base of Sangre de Cristo Mts. Follow graveled road from State Highway 17, 13 miles north of Alamosa (accommodations). Nature trail; campground.

Other sand-dune areas you may wish to see:

Monahans Sands, near Monahans, on U.S. 80, western Tex.
Pink Sands, northwest of Kanab, Utah.
Desert Sands, along U.S. 80, west of Yuma, Ariz.
Puerco Sands, on U.S. 60 and 85, north of Socorro, N. Mex.
In Death Valley National Monument, Calif.

CARLSBAD CAVERNS, in southeastern New Mexico, are world-famous for their immense size, their vaulted rooms, and their splendid natural formations. Park Service guided tours are conducted along 4 miles of underground paths. Formed by collapse of rock after slow solution, and decorated by limestone dripping, the caverns have been millions of years in the making. Changes in climate have long since made most of Carlsbad a "dead" cave. It was first explored by a cowboy, Jim White, about 1901. Hoards of harmless bats which live in an upper corridor pour from the natural entrance each summer evening. Twenty-one miles from the city of Carlsbad a paved highway to the park joins U.S. 62 and 180 from El Paso, Tex. Rail and air lines to El Paso or Carlsbad connect with buses to the Caverns. No overnight accommodations. Light meals.

Other Southwest caves you may wish to see:
Lehman Caves, Baker, Nev.
Colossal Cave, Vail (near Tucson), Ariz.
Cave of the Winds, Colorado Springs, Colo.
Whipple Cave, Cave Valley, Nev.
Crystal Cave, Oracle, Ariz.
Mitchell's Cave, Essex, Calif.

METEOR CRATER, a hole 570 ft. deep and more than ¾ mile wide, was blasted out some 50,000 years ago by the impact of a huge cluster of meteorites. The crater, 20 miles west of Winslow, Ariz., is most effectively seen from the air but may be reached by a 6-mile paved detour from U.S. 66. A small museum (admission fee) on the rim tells the story of meteor craters and displays meteoric materials. Accommodations at Winslow. Other meteor craters are near Odessa, Tex., and Haviland, Kan.

SUNSET CRATER, most recently active Southwest volcano, was formed about 1066 A.D., according to growth rings in timbers of Indian homes buried by its cinders. The crater lies in a symmetrical 1,000-ft. cinder cone surrounded by spectacular squeeze-ups, spatter cones, and lava flows. Proclaimed a national monument in 1930, the area is reached by a short road leaving U.S. 89 northeast of Flagstaff, Ariz. (accommodations here).

VOLCANIC PLUGS, such as Shiprock in northwestern New Mexico, are remnants of old volcanoes, whose dying throats were choked with cooling lava. Erosion of the volcanoes has left hard lava cores standing.

Plug: Shiprock

VOLCANIC DIKES may be large mountains, as Mt. Blanca, Colo.; or long lines of "hogbacks"; or vertical veins across country, as at Alamillo Creek, N. Mex., and below the volcanic Spanish Peaks near La Veta, Colo.

Dikes: Alamillo Creek

LAVA FLOWS, many old, some recent, are common. Best known are flows near Carrizozo and Grants, N. Mex.—the latter famous for perpetual ice caves near Paxton Springs. Other lava-flow ice caves are on Sierra Negra and Johnson Mesa between Folsom and Raton, N. Mex.

CALDERAS, cones of volcanoes that have blown off their tops, are rare in the Southwest. Valle Grande, in Jemez (HAY-mez) Mountains, N. Mex., is 18 miles across. It is surrounded by lava beds and compressed volcanic ash called "tuff."

Other volcanic plugs: Cabazon Peak, N. Mex.; Agathai Peak, Monument Valley; Lizard Head, near Telluride, Colo.; Huerfano Butte, near Walsenburg, Colo. Other cinder cones: Vulcan's Throne, in Grand Canyon National Monument; El Tintero, near Bluewater, N. Mex.; Capulin Mountain, near Capulin, N. Mex.; Ubehebe Crater, Death Valley National Monument; numerous cones near Springerville, Ariz.

Delicate Arch

ARCHES NATIONAL MONUMENT Arches may be defined as passages through obstructions, whereas natural bridges are passages that go over obstructions. In eastern Utah, near Moab, erosion has left many thin vertical slabs or fins of sandstone. Weathering sometimes perforates such fins to form windows. Enlargement of the openings results in stone arches. More than 80 such natural arches, some of them immense, are found in Arches National Monument. Mingled with them are balanced rocks, pinnacles, rock figures resembling men and animals, and a rugged area of brilliant red-banded rock called Fiery Furnace. A state highway enters the monument, leaving U.S. 160 at a point 4 miles north of Moab, where there are tourist accommodations. Leave trailers outside, as the monument road contains dips and steep grades. A picnic ground and self-guiding nature trail are available.

Other natural arches that may be on your route:

Window Rock, near the town of that name, Ariz.
Golden Arch, Organ Pipe Cactus National Monument, Ariz.
Cassidy's Arch, Capitol Reef National Monument, Utah.
Angel's Window, Cape Royal, Grand Canyon National Park, Ariz.
Arch Canyon and Hole-in-Rock, near San Juan River, southeastern Utah.

Owachomo Bridge

NATURAL BRIDGES NATIONAL MONUMENT, 50 miles by dirt road from Blanding, Utah, contains three huge natural stone spans forming a rough triangle 3 miles on a side. The entrance road ends in a small campground, from which a trail, with self-guiding markers, leads to Owachomo Bridge. There are no other facilities. Bring food, water, and camping equipment.

RAINBOW BRIDGE, world-famous, is hidden deep in the remote, rugged slickrock country west of Navajo Mountain in south-central Utah. Large enough to straddle the nation's capitol, it is dwarfed by its surroundings. It is reached by a 14-mile trail from Rainbow Lodge or Navajo Mountain Trading Post. Horses may be obtained. Only hardy outdoors people should attempt the trip. Boat travelers on the Colorado River hike 6 miles up Forbidden Canyon to Rainbow Bridge.

Other natural bridges:

Gregory—Escalante Wilderness, Utah.
Grosvenor—Escalante Wilderness, Utah.
White Mesa—near Inscription House Trading Post, Ariz.
Hickman—in Capitol Reef National Monument, Utah.
Travertine—near Pine, Ariz.
"Whopper" (unnamed)—Zion National Park, Utah.
Bryce—Bryce Canyon National Park, Utah.

Rainbow Bridge

Cliff Palace Ruin

MESA VERDE NATIONAL PARK, in extreme southwestern Colorado, containing the largest concentration of prehistoric cave village ruins in the United States, is one of the best places to see the handiwork of early Americans. In the park is a unique museum where the arts ana crafts of prehistoric Indians are exhibited and explained. Self-guided tours, conducted trips to the ruins, and campfire talks by Park Service archeologists tell the story of the Indians who farmed the mesas for 1,300 years. Major ruins are reached by paved roads. Horses may be hired for trail trips. The park is open all the year, but overnight accommodations and meals are available only during summer and early fall. There is a large campground. Enter the park midway between Mancos and Cortez, Colo., on U.S. 160.

Other Southwest cliff ruins:

Gila Cliff Dwellings National Monument, Silver City, N. Mex.
Bandelier National Monument, near Los Alamos, N. Mex.
Puye Cliff Ruins, near Santa Clara Pueblo, N. Mex.
Walnut Canyon National Monument, near Flagstaff, Ariz.

NAVAJO NATIONAL MONUMENT, in north-central Arizona, protects three spectacular cliff ruins. None is accessible by automobile; Betatakin is seen from a short trail near headquarters. Guide service, a campground, and Indian ponies are available. Dirt roads; be prepared to camp.

CANYON DE CHELLY (de-SHAY) **NATIONAL MONUMENT,** in northeastern Arizona has spectacular canyons containing ruins. White House Ruin is seen from the road; others are reached by hiking, horseback, or special automobile. Small museum, and guest ranch accommodations.

MONTEZUMA CASTLE NATIONAL MONUMENT, near the center of Arizona, is a spectacular cliff ruin easily reached by paved road. Ranger-archeologist guides and a museum describe prehistoric Indians of Verde Valley. Near Montezuma Well. Accommodations nearby.

TONTO NATIONAL MONUMENT, overlooking Roosevelt Reservoir, Ariz., is reached over unpaved but scenic Apache Trail. Gem-like cliff ruins are near. A museum, conducted trips, and a self-guiding trail tell of prehistoric Indians. Motels in Globe and other nearby towns.

AZTEC RUINS NATIONAL MONUMENT, on the west bank of the Animas River near Aztec, N. Mex., is an ancient village site used by prehistoric farmer Indians (not Aztecs). A small museum and trips through the ruins explain their activities and habits. Accommodations in Aztec and other towns.

CASA GRANDE NATIONAL MONUMENT, on State Highway 87, is the site of a ruined four-story earthen tower (p. 22) dominating a Hohokam walled village. A museum and a guided trip through the ruin tell of an early people who irrigated and farmed parts of the Gila Valley of Arizona.

TUZIGOOT NATIONAL MONUMENT, 3 miles east of Clarkdale in Arizona's Verde Valley, is the remnant of an Indian village on a hilltop. A museum exhibits prehistoric pottery, stone and bone tools, ancient jewelry. A self-guiding trail explains the ruin. Nearby towns offer accommodations. Jerome, a ghost town, is near.

WUPATKI NATIONAL MONUMENT contains the largest ruin among 800 prehistoric Indian homesites. Soil here was enriched by the eruption of Sunset Crater (see p. 130). The entrance road leaves U.S. 89 30 miles north of Flagstaff, Ariz. (accommodations). Self-guiding trails.

Pueblo Bonito Ruin

CHACO CANYON NATIONAL MONUMENT, in northwestern New Mexico, with a dozen great open-site ruins and hundreds of smaller sites, represents the highest development of prehistoric Pueblo Indian civilization in the Southwest. Superior masonry, a rich variety of stone and bone tools, pottery, and fabrics found in the ruins mark a peak of prehistoric culture. Midway between Thoreau, on U.S. 66, and Aztec, on State Highway 44, Chaco Canyon is reached over winding State Highway 56, sometimes made impassable by sand or mud. A campground, small museum, and guide service to Pueblo Bonito (Beautiful Village) are available. This ruin of over 830 rooms was explored by the National Geographic Society, 1921-27. Nearest facilities are 64 miles away.

Other open-site ruins that you may wish to see:
Bandelier National Monument, near Los Alamos, N. Mex.
Coronado State Monument, near Bernalillo, N. Mex.
Pecos State Monument, near Pecos, N. Mex.
Besh-ba-gowah Ruin, Globe, Ariz.
Pueblo Grande, Phoenix, Ariz.
Kinishba Ruin, near Fort Apache, Ariz.
Point of Pines Ruin, east of San Carlos, Ariz.
Hovenweep National Monument, west of Cortez, Colo.
Kiva Ruins, near McNary, Ariz.
Elden Pueblo, near Flagstaff, Ariz.

Old Walpi

HOPI INDIAN VILLAGES, high on protected tablelands west of Keams Canyon, Ariz., overlook the Painted Desert (see pp. 31 and 126). For eight centuries the Hópita (peaceful) people have occupied three fingers of Black Mesa, known (east to west) as First, Second, and Third Mesas. Visitors are welcome in the villages but should remember that the houses are private homes, not business places. Ceremonial dances are held frequently, the Soyabina opening the kachina program in December. In January there are hunting dances; in February, bean-sprouting dances; and during the summer, butterfly dances. Most famous is the Snake Dance held late in August. Although the main road through the Hopi country is now paved, side roads are dirt or gravel and may become difficult following rains. Trading posts offer gasoline and supplies but few overnight accommodations. Travelers off main roads may have to camp. See map on p. 31.

First Mesa Villages (People Make Pottery)	Second Mesa Villages (People Make Coiled Baskets)	Third Mesa Villages (People Make Twined Plaques)
Walpi	Mishongnovi	Oraibi
Sichomovi	Shipaulovi	Hotevilla
Hano	Shongopovi	Bacabi

HAVASUPAI Indians, a dwindling tribe, live in Supai Village, deep in Havasu Canyon, within Grand Canyon. Leave your car at Hilltop, on the canyon rim, and hike 14 miles to Supai; or, arrange to be met at Hilltop by Indians with saddle ponies. Blue-green water, three majestic waterfalls, and subtropical plants make the canyon a paradise. Limited accommodations at Supai Village.

QUIJOTOA (key-ho-TOE-ah), typical Papago Indian village, is in the desert northwest of Sells, Ariz., on State Highway 86. One-room mud-floored houses are of Saguaro ribs or Ocotillo stems plastered with mud. Come in spring or fall. At Sells are a Papago museum, store, and filling station. Meals and accommodations at Nogales, Tucson, Casa Grande, and other nearby centers.

ACOMA (AK-oh-mah), New Mexico's "Sky City," tops a small mesa, 14 miles by graveled road from U.S. 66 near San Fidel. It and Oraibi (p. 138) are called the oldest continuously occupied villages in the U.S. Acoma is reached by a steep foot trail winding up Acoma Rock. There is a charge for entering the pueblo, and a fee for taking photographs. Accommodations along U.S. 66.

SAN JOSE DE TUMACACORI started as a simple shelter in which the famous Spanish priest, Father Kino, said mass for the Sobaipuri Indians in 1691. By 1773 it had become a major mission. When, in 1844, Mexico sold the mission lands, Indians of the Tumacacori congregation moved the church furnishings to San Xavier (p. 141), near Tucson, Ariz. Abandoned, Tumacacori fell into ruin. In 1908 it was proclaimed a national monument and considerable work has since been done to stabilize the fine old building. A modern museum tells the story of Tumacacori and the Sonora chain of Kino Missions. U.S. 89 passes close to the walls. Tourist accommodations are available at Nogales, just below the Mexican border, 18 miles south; and in Tucson, 48 miles north.

Other old mission ruins you may wish to see:

Abo, Quarai, and Gran Quivira, near Mountainair, N. Mex.
Pecos and Jemez, near Santa Fe, N. Mex.
Quevavi, near Tumacacori, Ariz.
Quiburi, near Fairbank, Ariz.

SAN XAVIER (hah-VEER) was consecrated in 1797. Glistening white, combining Byzantine, Moorish, and Spanish architecture, it serves the Indians of Bac, 9 miles southwest of Tucson. Visitors welcome.

EL SANCTUARIO DE CHIMAYO, in a hamlet of blanket-weavers in the Santa Cruz Valley, northern N. Mex., dates from 1816. Quaint Spanish Pueblo. Pilgrims come here. Visit in early October.

SAN MIGUEL, in downtown Santa Fe, N. Mex. (p. 144), was built 1636, destroyed by Indians 1680, restored 1710. Now a chapel for St. Michael's School, it is periodically opened for public worship.

ST. FRANCIS OF ASSISI MISSION typifies the old Spanish Southwest. Center of ancient Ranchos de Taos, near Taos, N. Mex., it was a refuge in Apache and Comanche raids. Rebuilt 1772.

Other old churches and missions in New Mexico:

San Esteban Rey, Acoma Pueblo.
San Felipe de Nerí, Albuquerque.
San Miguel del Bado, San Miguel.
San Miguel Mission, Socorro.
Senora de los Dolores, Arroyo Hondo.
San José de Laguna, Laguna Pueblo.
Nuestra Señora de la Asunción, Zia Pueblo.
San Antonio de Isleta, Isleta Pueblo.

TOMBSTONE, Ariz., "The Town Too Tough to Die," typifies lusty, godless mining camps of early days. In its heyday, 1879-1885, Tombstone and its famous newspaper, *The Epitaph,* built a reputation that still draws visitors to wander among deserted gambling halls and explore the Birdcage Theater and Boothill Cemetery, where grimly humorous grave markers stand. Tombstone, on U.S. 80, is between Benson and Bisbee, which offer accommodations.

JEROME, rich in copper-mining lore, was born in 1882, died in 1952. For so young a ghost, it is amazingly famous—"The Most Unique Town in America." Its spectacular location on the face of Mingus Mountain, Ariz., puts it in the cliff-ruin class. Big Pit Mine and a modern museum are major attractions. U.S. 89A winds among abandoned buildings to Clarkdale, Cottonwood, and Prescott, all with accommodations. (Other ghost towns: see pp. 12; 42-43)

Fort Union National Monument

FORT UNION (1851-1891), at a junction of the Santa Fe Trail, was an army base. Adobe walls, guardhouse, brick chimneys, survive. Nine miles from Watrous on U.S. 85.

FORT DAVIS (1854-1891), in the Davis Mountains, western Texas (State Highways 17 and 118), was destroyed by Indians, rebuilt 1867. Garrisons fought Apaches and Comanches. Some buildings remain.

FORT BOWIE (1862-1896), near Apache Pass, Chiricahua Mountains, southeast Arizona, guarded stagecoaches and Gen. Nelson A. Miles' headquarters in the Geronimo campaign. Adobe walls remain on a spur from the Apache Pass road leaving U.S. 80 at Bowie (BOO-ee).

PIPE SPRING NATIONAL MONUMENT preserves a Mormon stone fort (1869-70) built around a spring. The fort protected colonists. On graded dirt road 15 miles southwest of Fredonia, northern Arizona.

Other old forts that may be visited (see map, pp. 42-43,also):

- Ft. Garland, Colo.
- Ft. Lyon, Colo.
- Ft. Bliss, Tex.
- Ft. Stockton, Tex.
- Ft. Huachuca, Ariz.
- Ft. Whipple, Ariz.
- Ft. Lowell, Ariz.
- Ft. McDowell, Ariz.
- Ft. Defiance, Ariz.
- Ft. Grant, Ariz.
- Ft. Stanton, N. Mex.
- Ft. Craig, N. Mex.
- Ft. Wingate, N. Mex.
- Ft. Sumner, N. Mex.
- Ft. Bayard, N. Mex.

Pipe Spring Fort

Santa Fe Claims the Oldest House in the U.S.

SANTA FE (City of the Holy Faith), capital of New Mexico, was the center of Spanish and Pueblo Indian culture and of Catholic activities during the mission period, when Jesuit and Franciscan priests were active. It is now a modern art and cultural center. Santa Fe's plaza, planned in Madrid, Spain, and built in 1609-1610, was the terminus of two great trails: the Camino Real from Vera Cruz, Mexico, first traveled in 1581; and the Santa Fe Trail, main route west from Independence, Mo., after 1821. North of the plaza is the Palace of the Governors, now a museum, over which have flown six flags. Nearby are the New Mexico Museum of Art and Cathedral of St. Francis. Highways lead to prehistoric Indian ruins, to modern Indian pueblos, and to native villages where Spanish is still the mother tongue. Locale of summer outdoor opera.

Other Spanish-American towns (all but the first two in New Mexico) that retain native character:

San Luis, Colo.
Nogales, Ariz.
Cordova
Socorro
Abiquiu
Mesilla
Tecolote
San José
Penasco
Truchas
Tierra Amarilla
Bernalillo
Cundiyo
Mora
Pecos

MUSEUMS containing scientific or historical collections and educational displays are numerous in the Southwest. Many national parks and monuments provide exhibits as aids in understanding the features they protect. Outstanding among these are the early Indian exhibits at Mesa Verde, the Yavapai Point Station explaining the major geological and biological stories illustrated in the Grand Canyon, and the Spanish Mission exhibits at Tumacacori, Ariz. Displays at the University of Arizona, Tucson, outline the story of prehistoric man in the Southwest. Private institutions, such as the Heard Museum at Phoenix, the Museum of Northern Arizona at Flagstaff, and the Barringer Meteor Crater Museum (*) west of Winslow, Ariz., are of particular interest to travelers.

Other museums (* admission fee) you may wish to see:

Pioneer Village, Las Vegas, Nev.
*Lost City Museum, Overton, Nev.
San Jacinto Museum, San Jacinto Monument, Tex.
Panhandle-Plains Historical Museum, Canyon, Tex.
Sul Ross Historical Museum, Alpine, Tex.
Utah Historical Museum, Fillmore, Utah.
Taylor Museum and Fine Arts Center, Colorado Springs, Colo.
*Nininger Meteorite Museum, Sedona, Ariz.
Mineral Museum, State Fair Grounds, Phoenix, Ariz.
*Museum of Mining History, Jerome, Ariz.
Archeological Museum of the University of New Mexico, Albuquerque
Museum of International Folk Art, Santa Fe, N. Mex.
*Museum of Navajo Ceremonial Art, Santa Fe, N. Mex.

(For other museums, see pp. 45-47.)

Governors' Palace, Santa Fe

DEATH VALLEY NATIONAL MONUMENT, Calif., established 1933, features scenery, geology, unique desert life, and the lowest spot in the Western Hemisphere, 282 ft. below sea level. Accommodations: campground, hotels, motels. Climate: ideal October-April. Paved routes: from Baker, Calif.; Beatty, Nev.; Lone Pine or Olancha, Calif. Furnace Creek has a small airport. Las Vegas, Nev., is the nearest railhead.

ORGAN PIPE CACTUS NATIONAL MONUMENT, southwestern Ariz., near Mexico, protects many semi-tropical plants and animals not found elsewhere in the U.S. After winters of above-average rainfall, a mass of flowers appears, then trees, shrubs, and cactuses bloom. A highway leaving State Highway 86, 12 miles south of Ajo (AH-hoe), crosses the monument en route to the Gulf of California. A store at Lukeville and a campground offer the only accommodations nearer than Ajo.

Joshua Tree Forests occur near Pierce Ferry, Ariz.; on State Highway 93 northwest of Congress, Ariz.; and in Joshua Tree National Monument, between Twentynine Palms and Indio, Calif. Largest of yuccas (p. 90), this tree is spectacular in bloom, late February to early April.

Arizona-Sonora Desert Museum, 12 miles northwest of Tucson, in a forest of Giant Cactus, exhibits desert plants and animals. Labels tell about each species and the part it plays in the desert community. Attendants answer questions.

Desert Botanical Gardens of Arizona display desert plants in Papago Park between Phoenix and Tempe (tem-PEE). Lectures are given. Plants are sold. Also try Boyce Thompson Southwest Arboretum, near Superior, Ariz.

Saguaro (suh-WAR-oh) **National Monument** displays many desert plants and animals. Markers and a leaflet explain features along a 9-mile loop drive. Small picnic ground and museum. Tucson (17 miles west) has modern accommodations.

DESERT AGRICULTURE, based on irrigation, goes back at least 1,000 years in the Southwest. Irrigation systems now distribute water from huge reservoirs and thousands of deep wells to millions of arid acres (see p. 48). Fertile soils and a long growing season (up to 355 days) produce enormous crops of alfalfa, cereals, cotton, vegetables, citrus fruits, and dates. Winter crops include head lettuce, wheat, and carrots. Cantaloupes ripen early, and cotton is king of the field crops. Most of the alfalfa, hegari, corn, and similar crops are fed to range cattle to condition them for market. Sugar beets, figs, olives, pecans, and honey are among the specialized crops of the desert.

Some of the agricultural centers you will want to visit:

Yuma, Ariz.: Citrus, dates, pecans, alfalfa, wheat, grapes.
Phoenix, Ariz.: Citrus, alfalfa, cotton, vegetables.
Coolidge, Ariz.: Cotton, carrots, alfalfa, hegari.
Las Cruces, N. Mex.: Cotton, alfalfa, hegari.
Hobbs, N. Mex.: Berries, vegetables, grapes.
El Paso, Tex.: Cotton, alfalfa.
Monte Vista, Colo.: Potatoes, alfalfa, honey.
Grand Junction, Colo.: Apples, peaches, pears, cherries, alfalfa.
Imperial Valley, Calif.: Sugar beets, tobacco, lettuce, celery, tomatoes, cotton, dates.

Deep-well Irrigation

WILDLIFE REFUGES are for the protection of wild creatures, which, like men, must have a place to live, natural food, shelter, and a suitable environment to raise families. By protecting native wildlife in its environment, federal and state agencies provide an enormous impetus to human recreation. In the refuges, native animals may be seen, photographed, and studied. In some, overnight accommodations are available for visitors. All national parks and monuments are wildlife refuges. State parks and monuments also protect wildlife. National Wildlife Refuges of the U.S. Fish and Wildlife Service include the following:

Wichita Mountains National Wildlife Refuge, near Lawton, Okla.: Buffalo, deer, turkeys, longhorn cattle. Campsites.
Salt Plains National Wildlife Refuge, near Cherokee, Okla.
Muleshoe National Wildlife Refuge, northwest of Lubbock, Tex.
Bitter Lake Migratory Waterfowl Refuge, near Roswell, N. Mex.
Bosque del Apache National Wildlife Refuge, at head of Elephant Butte Reservoir, N. Mex.: Waterfowl and fishing.
San Andreas National Wildlife Refuge, west of White Sands National Monument, N. Mex.
Safford National Wildlife Refuge, near Safford, Ariz.
Salt River National Wildlife Refuge, near Roosevelt, Ariz.
Cabeza Prieta Game Refuge, adjoining Organ Pipe Cactus National Monument, Ariz.: Desert Bighorn and Peccary.
Kofa Game Refuge, near Yuma, Ariz.: Desert Bighorn.
Imperial and Havasu National Wildlife Refuge, near Yuma, Ariz.
Desert Game Range, near Las Vegas, Nev.
Salton Sea National Wildlife Refuge, at south end of Salton Sea, Calif.

For further information, write U.S. Fish and Wildlife Service, P. O. Box 1306, Albuquerque, N. Mex.

HOOVER DAM (formerly **BOULDER DAM**), completed 1936, is the highest (726 ft.) on the Colorado River. It formed Lake Mead—115 miles long, 229 square miles. Surrounded by desert, Lake Mead National Recreation Area provides swimming, boating, fishing. The dam's generators and mazes of corridors are reached by elevators. Dept. of Interior guides explain equipment and construction. The dam's crescent top is a broad highway, 1,282 ft. long, linking Arizona with Nevada. A museum at the Nevada end depicts the immense territory served with water and power by the dam. Other dams that create reservoirs along the Colorado River are Davis, Parker, Imperial, and Laguna Dams. Accommodations: Boulder City, Nev., 6 miles west, and Las Vegas, Nev., 29 miles northwest, of Hoover Dam.

Hoover Dam

GREAT DAMS impound water, generate electricity, harness destructive flood forces of the three big rivers of the Southwest—Colorado, Rio Grande, and Arkansas. Dams of the Southwest have contradicted climatic laws and stimulated westward expansion. Roosevelt Dam (completed 1911), 60 miles northeast of Phoenix, Ariz., started the reclamation parade. It is in the center of a scenic area tapped by State Highway 88 (Apache Trail), which also passes four other large dams and the 59-mile chain of lakes on the Salt River. Arizona's Verde River boasts Horseshoe and Bartlett Dams, and Coolidge Dam is the main structure on the Gila. Elephant Butte and Caballo are the big dams on the Rio Grande in New Mexico.

Other dams you may see in the Southwest:

Bluewater, in the Zuni Mountains, near Bluewater, N. Mex.
Alamogordo, on the Pecos River, near Fort Sumner, N. Mex.
Avalon, on the Pecos, near Carlsbad, N. Mex.
Conchas, on the Canadian, near Tucumcari, N. Mex.
Eagle Nest, on the Cimarron, near Taos, N. Mex.
El Vado, on the Chama, near Park View, N. Mex.
McMillan, on the Pecos, near Lakewood, N. Mex.
John Martin, on the Arkansas, near Fort Lyon, Colo.
Carl Pleasant, on the Agua Fria, near Peoria, Ariz.
Gillespie, on the Hassayampa, near Buckeye, Ariz.

OPEN-PIT COPPER MINES are spectacular large-scale diggings; many pock the Southwest. A visit to any one, particularly during operations, is memorable. Mines are seen at Ajo, Bisbee, Jerome, Morenci, and Clifton, in Arizona; Santa Rita, near Silver City, N. Mex., and the Ruth Pit, near Ely, Nev. There are smelters at Douglas, Miami, Globe, Hayden, Ariz., and El Paso, Tex.

GOLD AND SILVER are often found with copper. Gold mining is active near Oatman, Ariz. Extensive potash workings underlie southeastern New Mexico near Carlsbad. Silver, lead, and zinc are mined near Pioche, Nev. Uranium ore occurs in S.E. Utah, S.W. Colo., and near Grants, New Mexico. Trinidad, Colo., and Raton, Gallup, and Madrid, New Mexico were once coal-mining centers, now superseded by petroleum and natural-gas production. For other minerals see pp. 113-114.

NATURAL-GAS AND OIL production is growing. Fields are being developed in western Texas and northwestern New Mexico. The Hobbs Field, in southeastern N. Mex., and one north of Pecos., Tex., afford sightseeing opportunities for travelers on main highways. Oil discoveries in eastern Nevada are reported. Helium, the rare nonflammable gas, occurs in several Southwestern oil fields, and a helium extracting and bottling plant is located just west of Amarillo, Tex., on U.S. 66.

NATURAL HOT SPRINGS, mainly of mineralized water, are used for therapeutic purposes. Such springs, in various degrees of development, dot the Southwest. Many are maintained by privately owned health resorts and guest ranches. Those at Truth or Consequences and Ojo Caliente, N. Mex., are well known. Other hot springs of interest include:

Verde Hot Springs, Ariz.
Agua Caliente Hot Springs, Ariz.
Indian Hot Springs,
  Thatcher, Ariz.
Tonopah Hot Springs,
  Buckeye, Ariz.
Castle Hot Springs,
  Morristown, Ariz.
Clifton Hot Springs, Clifton, Ariz.
Monroe Hot Springs,
  Monroe, Utah.
Jemez Springs, N. Mex.
Frisco Hot Springs,
  Luna, N. Mex.
Faywood Hot Springs,
  Faywood, N. Mex.
In Big Bend National Park, Tex.
Spencer Hot Springs,
  Austin, Nev.
Warm Springs, Nev.
Mineral Hot Springs,
  Saguache (sy-WATCH), Colo.

HUNTING AND FISHING is "big business" in the Southwest. Vast areas of sparsely populated land suitable for native animals, large bodies of water behind the great irrigation dams (see p. 151), and expert management by game and fish commissions of the various states have combined to maintain a dependable population of fish and game. This is harvested by local sportsmen and vacationers, hunters, and fishermen from other regions. Pack trips into the high country usually yield larger bags because there is less pressure on game species in areas inaccessible to automobiles. License fees, open seasons, and bag limits vary in different states and from year to year. Sportsmen should consult local game wardens or the state game warden's office.

Some of the most widely sought game in the Southwest:

Game Mammals

- Mule Deer
- White-tail Deer
- Bear
- Elk
- Antelope
- Bison
- Bighorn
- Peccary
- Rabbits

Game Birds

- Mourning Dove
- White-winged Dove
- Gambel and Blue Quail
- Chukar
- Sage and Dusky Grouse
- Prairie Chicken
- Pheasants
- Wild Turkey
- Wild Ducks and Geese

MOUNTAIN CLIMBING is for youth, but many "oldsters" are addicts, too. Wooded foothills with graded trails; rugged 13,000- to 14,000-ft. peaks; crags and cliffs requiring ropes, pitons, and all the know-how of scientific mountaineering — the Southwest has them all. Colorado alone has 52 peaks of 14,000 ft. or more. Persons unaccustomed to mountain-climbing should be wary of over-exertion and falls.

SKIING, universal winter sport, is popular in the Southwest. High mountains with north slopes catch and hold snow until late spring. Popular ski runs, most with rope tows or chair lifts, include:

In Colorado: Aspen, Wolf Creek Pass, South Park, and Gunnison. **In Utah:** Cedar City and Beaver. **In Nevada:** Mt. Charleston, near Las Vegas. **In New Mexico:** Cloudcroft; Raton; Madera; Albuquerque; Tres Ritos; Taos; and Aspen Basin, Santa Fe. **In Arizona:** Arizona Snow Bowl, Flagstaff; Upper Sabino Canyon, Tucson; Bill Williams, Williams; Mingus Mountain, Jerome; and Saint Agathe, near Prescott.

Other skiing centers in the Southwest (see also p. 5):

Mt. Whitney, Calif., 14,495 ft.
Mt. Elbert, Colo., 14,431 ft.
Kings Peak, Utah, 13,498 ft.
Wheeler Peak, N. Mex., 13,151 ft.
Boundary Peak, Nev., 13,145 ft.
Humphreys Peak, Ariz., 12,655 ft.

OTHER INTERESTING PLACES

TRIPS: Boat Trips on Colorado River; rugged, primitive; from Marble Canyon Ariz., Mexican Hat, or Green River, Utah.

D.&R.G.W. Narrow-gage Railroad—Durango to Silverton, Colo., only road of its kind in U.S.

"Trail Riders of the Wilderness" Pack Trips—Write American Forestry Assoc., 917-17th St. N.W., Washington 6, D. C. Similar pack trips may be arranged with local guides.

"Million Dollar Highway"—Ouray to Durango, Colo.; rugged.

"Four Corners" (only place in U.S. where four states meet) **and Goosenecks of San Juan, Colo.**

Inner Grand Canyon Trails—Muleback or foot. Primitive roads to Grand Canyon Nat. Mon., Ariz.

Deep-sea Fishing—Gulf of California at Punta Peñasco, 60 miles south of border, from Organ Pipe Cactus Nat. Mon., Ariz. Other trips into Mexico from border cities: Juárez, Sonoita, Nogales, Mexicali, Agua Prieta, etc.

PLACES: Astronomical observatories—McDonald at Ft. Davis, Tex.; Lowell at Flagstaff, Ariz.; Palomar and Mt. Wilson in Calif.

Other National and State Parks and Monuments—Write to National Park Service, Box 1728, Santa Fe, N. Mex., and to state capitals.

National Forests—Write to Regional Forester, U.S. Forest Service, Federal Building, Albuquerque, N. Mex. for list.

Los Alamos, N. Mex.—Atom Bomb City. Visitors welcome.

Navajo Indian Reservation—Check road conditions first.

Mormon Temples—St. George and Manti, Utah; Mesa, Ariz. No admittance, but beautiful buildings from outside.

Salton Sea and Imperial Valley, Calif.

ACTIVITIES TO WATCH: Logging at Flagstaff, Ariz. Cattle-ranching (branding, roundups, etc.) in many areas.

Football Games—Sun Bowl, El Paso; Salad Bowl, Phoenix.

Rocket and Guided-missile Tests—White Sands Proving Grounds, N. Mex. (No admittance; observe from a distance.)

INDEX

Asterisks (*) denote pages on which the subjects are illustrated.